Everything the Bible Says About
HEAVEN

BETHANYHOUSE
Minneapolis, Minnesota

© 2011 by Bethany House Publishers

Compiled by Linda Washington
Series editors: Kyle Duncan and Andy McGuire

Published by Bethany House Publishers
11400 Hampshire Avenue South
Bloomington, Minnesota 55438
www.bethanyhouse.com

Bethany House Publishers is a division of
Baker Publishing Group, Grand Rapids, Michigan

Printed in the United States of America

Library of Congress Cataloging-in-Publication Data is available for this title.

Cover design by Eric Walljasper

16   17   18   19   20   21   9   8   7   6   5   4

Everything the
Bible Says About
HEAVEN

CONTENTS

INTRODUCTION   7

CHAPTER 1
The Place Where God Dwells: Old Testament
Visions of Heaven   9

CHAPTER 2
Many Mansions: New Testament Visions of
Heaven   31

CHAPTER 3
Heaven in the Book of Revelation   51

CHAPTER 4
Between Heaven and Earth   73

CHAPTER 5
Answers From Heaven   85

CHAPTER 6
Who Will Go to Heaven?   95

NOTES   107

INTRODUCTION

Picture this: Millions of people seated on downy-soft clouds strumming harps for thousands of years. Sound inviting? Not really. But if you poll the average person, you'll find that many have this picture in mind when they think of heaven.

Movies like *Heaven Can Wait* (1978) and *Dogma* (1999) present this myopic view of heaven—a boring place where mistakes are made and fallen angels can gate-crash if they catch God in an error. Based on these scenarios, would *you* want to go to heaven?

In his novel *The Five People You Meet in Heaven*, Mitch Albom describes an eighty-three-year-old man (Eddie) who died and went to heaven. Eddie searches for the meaning of his life and a sense of redemption. In a way, this book is a lot like Frank Capra's classic movie *It's a Wonderful Life* (1946). But is *that* what heaven is really like?

Many who read older literature like *Pilgrim's Progress* by John Bunyan or *The Divine Comedy* by Dante Alighieri (specifically the *Paradiso* canto) have a different view of heaven—as a beautiful Celestial City or a realm with nine spheres. Milton's *Paradise Lost* details Satan's fall from heaven and then his temptation of man, which causes Adam and Eve to be cast out of Paradise. While these authors took fictional license in their descriptions of heaven, some of these descriptions are based on the Scriptures.

So what *is* heaven really like? What does the Bible have to say about heaven? This book has answers.

CHAPTER 1

The Place Where God Dwells: Old Testament Visions of Heaven

Tabitha was silent, thinking. Why must people always think of heaven as being up in the sky? Why should it be there more than anywhere else? The sky wasn't any more heavenly than the earth in springtime. Why shouldn't heaven be within half a mile of them?

—Elizabeth Goudge, *The Valley of Song*[1]

For many people living during Old Testament times, *heaven* was synonymous with *sky*—the canopy of air above their heads. The stars and star clusters, like the Pleiades, could be found there. But for many of God's people, heaven was God's dwelling place—a realm or kingdom in the sky. Angels also were inhabitants of heaven. Those who looked forward to the coming of the Messiah viewed heaven as a future habitation—the place of eternal rest. In heaven, a reunion with lost loved ones was possible.

Prophets like Moses, Isaiah, and Ezekiel were granted visions of heaven and saw sights beyond their understanding.

These glimpses of heaven show that God isn't merely "up there somewhere in the sky" but in a real place, enthroned in majesty.

And he blessed Abram, saying, "Blessed be Abram by God Most High, Creator of heaven and earth" **(GENESIS 14:19 NIV).**

This is the first time the Bible mentions "heaven" rather than "the heavens." Here Melchizedek, a priest-king, blesses Abram based on a title of God. This title is meant to describe an actual place rather than merely "the sky."

Then Moses and Aaron, Nadab, and Abihu, and seventy of the elders of Israel went up, and they saw the God of Israel. There was under his feet as it were a pavement of sapphire stone, like the very heaven for clearness. And he did not lay his hand on the chief men of the people of Israel; they beheld God, and ate and drank. **(EXODUS 24:9–11 ESV)**

I call heaven and earth to witness against you today that you will soon utterly perish from the land that you are crossing the Jordan to occupy; you will not live long on it, but will be utterly destroyed. **(DEUTERONOMY 4:26 NRSV)**

To underline the urgency of keeping the covenant, or promise, with God, Moses calls heaven and earth to witness the agreement. The testimony of two witnesses was necessary to decide a legal matter. Here, heaven and earth—two separate realms—are called to witness. (See also Deuteronomy 30:19.)

Look down from your holy habitation, from heaven, and bless your people Israel and the ground that you have given us, as you swore to our fathers, a land flowing with milk and honey. **(DEUTERONOMY 26:15 ESV)**

[David] said, "While the child was still alive, I fasted and wept, for I said, 'Who knows whether the LORD will be gracious to me, that the child may live?' But now he is dead. Why should I fast? Can I bring him back again? I shall go to him, but he will not return to me" **(2 SAMUEL 12:22–23 ESV)**.

After a child is conceived during David's sin with Bathsheba (2 Samuel 11), God sent a prophet to tell David that the child would die. Even in his grief, David had a sense of the afterlife, knowing that he would see his dead child again in heaven.

O LORD, God of Israel, there is no God like you in all of heaven above or on the earth below. You keep your covenant and show unfailing love to all who walk before you in wholehearted devotion. . . . But will God really live on earth? Why, even the highest heavens cannot contain you. How much less this Temple I have built! **(1 KINGS 8:23, 27 NLT)**

Solomon knows that all of God cannot be contained in a temple or even in heaven. God is omnipresent—he is everywhere.

Then Micaiah continued, "Listen to what the LORD says! I saw the LORD sitting on his throne with all the armies of heaven around him, on his right and on his left. And the LORD said, 'Who can entice Ahab to go into battle against Ramoth-gilead so he can be killed?'

"There were many suggestions, and finally a spirit approached the LORD and said, 'I can do it!'

"'How will you do this?' the LORD asked. And the spirit replied, 'I will go out and inspire all of Ahab's prophets to speak lies.'

"'You will succeed,' said the LORD. 'Go ahead and do it.' So you see, the LORD has put a lying spirit in the mouths of all your prophets. For the LORD has pronounced your doom" **(1 KINGS 22:19–23 NLT).**

The prophet Micaiah details his strange vision of heaven in response to the scoffing of Zedekiah, a lying prophet. Some view this vision merely as a literary device to make a point about lying prophets. Others see it as a literal vision of heaven. (See also 2 Chronicles 18:18–22.) The doom pronounced by God was that of Ahab, an evil king.

———— ♦ ————

Elisha replied, "Listen to this message from the LORD! This is what the LORD says: By this time tomorrow in the markets of Samaria, five quarts of choice flour will cost only one piece of silver, and ten quarts of barley grain will cost only one piece of silver." The officer assisting the king said to the man of God, "That couldn't happen even if the LORD opened the windows of heaven!" But Elisha replied, "You will see it happen with your own eyes, but you won't be able to eat any of it!" **(2 KINGS 7:1–2 NLT).**

The "windows of heaven" refer to a heavenly storehouse. This is another way of saying that God's resources are unlimited.

Now there was a day when the sons of God came to present themselves before the LORD, and Satan also came among them. The LORD said to Satan, "From where have you come?" Satan answered the LORD and said, "From going to and fro on the earth, and from walking up and down on it." And the LORD said to Satan, "Have you considered my servant Job, that there is none like him on the earth, a blameless and upright man, who fears God and turns away from evil?" Then Satan answered the LORD and said, "Does Job fear God for no reason? Have you not put a hedge around him and his house and all that he has, on every side? You have blessed the work of his hands, and his possessions have increased in the land. But stretch out your hand and touch all that he has, and he will curse you to your face." And the LORD said to Satan, "Behold, all that he has is in your hand. Only against him do not stretch out your hand." So Satan went out from the presence of the LORD. (JOB 1:6–12 ESV)

This conversation takes place in the beginning of the book of Job and describes the first of two tests of the righteous man. Satan appears before the throne of God in heaven, which shows that he still had access to heaven.

Again there was a day when the sons of God came to present themselves before the LORD, and Satan also came among them to present himself before the LORD.

The LORD said to Satan, "Where have you come from?" Then Satan answered the LORD and said, "From roaming about on the earth and walking around on it."

The LORD said to Satan, "Have you considered My servant Job? For there is no one like him on the earth, a blameless and upright man fearing God and turning away from evil.

And he still holds fast his integrity, although you incited Me against him to ruin him without cause."

Satan answered the LORD and said, "Skin for skin! Yes, all that a man has he will give for his life.

"However, put forth Your hand now, and touch his bone and his flesh; he will curse You to Your face."

So the LORD said to Satan, "Behold, he is in your power, only spare his life."

Then Satan went out from the presence of the LORD and smote Job with sore boils from the sole of his foot to the crown of his head. **(JOB 2:1–7 NASB).**

Is not God in the heights of heaven? And see how lofty are the highest stars! . . . Thick clouds veil him, so he does not see us as he goes about in the vaulted heavens. **(JOB 22:12, 14 NIV)**

Eliphaz the Temanite accuses Job of a wrong attitude toward God. Eliphaz asserts that Job believes God is so far away (in heaven) that he cannot understand Job's sufferings.

He holdeth back the face of his throne, and spreadeth his clouds upon it. . . . The pillars of heaven tremble and are astonished at his reproof. **(JOB 26:9, 11 KJV)**

Here Job describes God placing clouds throughout the sky. The "pillars of heaven" may refer to God's display of power.

The LORD is in his holy temple. The LORD's throne is in heaven. His eyes see. They examine Adam's descendants. **(PSALM 11:4 GOD'S WORD)**

———— ♦ ————

I have set the LORD continually before me; Because He is at my right hand, I will not be shaken. Therefore my heart is glad and my glory rejoices; my flesh also will dwell securely. For You will not abandon my soul to Sheol; nor will You allow Your Holy One to undergo decay. You will make known to me the path of life; in Your presence is fullness of joy; in Your right hand there are pleasures forever. **(PSALM 16:8–11 NASB)**

> *David looks forward to life after death. He knows that he will not go to Sheol, the place of torment. Instead, he will enjoy life forever with God.*

———— ♦ ————

In the year that King Uzziah died, I saw the Lord seated on a high and lofty throne, and His robe filled the temple. Seraphim were standing above Him; each one had six wings: with two he covered his face, with two he covered his feet, and with two he flew. And one called to another:

Holy, holy, holy is the LORD of Hosts; His glory fills the whole earth.

The foundations of the doorways shook at the sound of their voices, and the temple was filled with smoke.

Then I said: Woe is me, for I am ruined, because I am a man of unclean lips and live among a people of unclean lips, [and] because my eyes have seen the King, the LORD of Hosts.

Then one of the seraphim flew to me, and in his hand was a glowing coal that he had taken from the altar with tongs. He touched my mouth [with it] and said: Now that this has touched your lips, your wickedness is removed, and your sin is atoned for.

Then I heard the voice of the Lord saying: Who should I send? Who will go for Us?

I said: Here I am. Send me. **(ISAIAH 6:1–8 HCSB)**

During his call to be God's spokesman, Isaiah has a vision of the glory of God in the temple.

Out of the stump of David's family will grow a shoot—yes, a new Branch bearing fruit from the old root. And the Spirit of the Lord will rest on him—the Spirit of wisdom and understanding, the Spirit of counsel and might, the Spirit of knowledge and the fear of the Lord.

He will delight in obeying the Lord. He will not judge by appearance nor make a decision based on hearsay. He will give justice to the poor and make fair decisions for the exploited. The earth will shake at the force of his word, and one breath from his mouth will destroy the wicked. He will wear righteousness like a belt and truth like an undergarment.

In that day the wolf and the lamb will live together; the leopard will lie down with the baby goat. The calf and the yearling will be safe with the lion, and a little child will lead them all. The cow will graze near the bear. The cub and the calf will lie down together. The lion will eat hay like a cow. The baby will play safely near the hole of a cobra.

Yes, a little child will put its hand in a nest of deadly snakes without harm. Nothing will hurt or destroy in all my holy mountain, for as the waters fill the sea, so the earth will be filled with people who know the Lord. In that day the heir to David's throne will be a banner of salvation to all the world. The nations will rally to him, and the land where he lives will be a glorious place. **(ISAIAH 11:1–10 NLT)**

While some scholars see the animals mentioned above as metaphors for once-hostile nations that would become tame during Jesus' millennial kingdom, others see this as a prophecy of heaven through a restoration of the earth, including the animal kingdom.

How have you fallen from heaven, O light-bringer and day-star, son of the morning! How you have been cut down to the ground, you who weakened and laid low the nations [O blasphemous, satanic king of Babylon!]

And you said in your heart, I will ascend to heaven; I will exalt my throne above the stars of God; I will sit upon the mount of assembly in the uttermost north.

I will ascend above the heights of the clouds; I will make myself like the Most High.

Yet you shall be brought down to Sheol (Hades), to the innermost recesses of the pit (the region of the dead). **(ISAIAH 14:12–15 AMP)**

While this passage discusses the fate of the king of Babylon, many scholars believe that Isaiah also describes the fall of Satan (Lucifer) from heaven. "Daystar" or "morning star" represent the Latin for Lucifer.

Your gates will stay open around the clock to receive the wealth of many lands. The kings of the world will be led as captives in a victory procession. For the nations that refuse to serve you will be destroyed. The glory of Lebanon will be yours—the forests of cypress, fir, and pine—to beautify my sanctuary. My Temple will be glorious! The descendants of your tormentors will come and bow before you. Those who despised you will kiss your feet. They will call you the City of the Lord, and Zion of the Holy One of Israel.

Though you were once despised and hated, with no one traveling through you, I will make you beautiful forever, a joy to all generations. Powerful kings and mighty nations will satisfy your every need, as though you were a child nursing at the breast of a queen. You will know at last that I, the LORD, am your Savior and your Redeemer, the Mighty One of Israel.

I will exchange your bronze for gold, your iron for silver, your wood for bronze, and your stones for iron. I will make peace your leader and righteousness your ruler. Violence will disappear from your land; the desolation and destruction of war will end. Salvation will surround you like city walls, and praise will be on the lips of all who enter there.

No longer will you need the sun to shine by day, nor the moon to give its light by night, for the LORD your God will be your everlasting light, and your God will be your glory.

Your sun will never set; your moon will not go down. For the LORD will be your everlasting light. Your days of mourning will come to an end. All your people will be righteous. They will possess their land forever, for I will plant them there with my own hands in order to bring myself glory. The smallest family will become a thousand people, and the tiniest group will become a mighty nation. At the right time, I, the LORD, will make it happen. (ISAIAH 60:11–22 NLT)

Isaiah prophesied an encouraging message to his people. This passage speaks beyond even the future restoration of Israel to their land after the predicted exile. This is a picture of New Jerusalem—the heavenly city of Revelation 21.

Look! I am creating new heavens and a new earth, and no one will even think about the old ones anymore. Be glad; rejoice forever in my creation! And look! I will create Jerusalem as a place of happiness. Her people will be a source of joy. I will rejoice over Jerusalem and delight in my people. And the sound of weeping and crying will be heard in it no more. **(ISAIAH 65:17–19 NLT)**

They will come home and sing songs of joy on the heights of Jerusalem. They will be radiant because of the Lord's good gifts—the abundant crops of grain, new wine, and olive oil, and the healthy flocks and herds. Their life will be like a watered garden, and all their sorrows will be gone. The young women will dance for joy, and the men—old and young—will join in the celebration. I will turn their mourning into joy. I will comfort them and exchange their sorrow for rejoicing. The priests will enjoy abundance, and my people will feast on my good gifts. I, the Lord, have spoken! **(JEREMIAH 31:12–14 NLT)**

> *While the return of the exiles fulfilled a portion of Jeremiah's prophecy, the full extent of the promise will not be realized until heaven.*

As I looked, behold, a storm wind was coming from the north, a great cloud with fire flashing forth continually and a bright light around it, and in its midst something like glowing metal in the midst of the fire.

Within it there were figures resembling four living beings. And this was their appearance: they had human form.

Each of them had four faces and four wings. Their legs

were straight and their feet were like a calf's hoof, and they gleamed like burnished bronze.

Under their wings on their four sides were human hands. As for the faces and wings of the four of them, their wings touched one another; their faces did not turn when they moved, each went straight forward.

As for the form of their faces, each had the face of a man; all four had the face of a lion on the right and the face of a bull on the left, and all four had the face of an eagle.

Such were their faces. Their wings were spread out above; each had two touching another being, and two covering their bodies.

And each went straight forward; wherever the spirit was about to go, they would go, without turning as they went.

In the midst of the living beings there was something that looked like burning coals of fire, like torches darting back and forth among the living beings. The fire was bright, and lightning was flashing from the fire.

And the living beings ran to and fro like bolts of lightning.

Now as I looked at the living beings, behold, there was one wheel on the earth beside the living beings, for each of the four of them.

The appearance of the wheels and their workmanship was like sparkling beryl, and all four of them had the same form, their appearance and workmanship being as if one wheel were within another.

Whenever they moved, they moved in any of their four directions without turning as they moved.

As for their rims they were lofty and awesome, and the rims of all four of them were full of eyes round about.

Whenever the living beings moved, the wheels moved with them. And whenever the living beings rose from the earth, the wheels rose also.

Wherever the spirit was about to go, they would go in that direction. And the wheels rose close beside them; for the spirit of the living beings was in the wheels.

Whenever those went, these went; and whenever those stood still, these stood still. And whenever those rose from the earth, the wheels rose close beside them; for the spirit of the living beings was in the wheels.

Now over the heads of the living beings there was something like an expanse, like the awesome gleam of crystal, spread out over their heads.

Under the expanse their wings were stretched out straight, one toward the other; each one also had two wings covering its body on the one side and on the other.

I also heard the sound of their wings like the sound of abundant waters as they went, like the voice of the Almighty, a sound of tumult like the sound of an army camp; whenever they stood still, they dropped their wings.

And there came a voice from above the expanse that was over their heads; whenever they stood still, they dropped their wings.

Now above the expanse that was over their heads there was something resembling a throne, like lapis lazuli in appearance; and on that which resembled a throne, high up, was a figure with the appearance of a man.

Then I noticed from the appearance of His loins and upward something like glowing metal that looked like fire all around within it, and from the appearance of His loins and downward I saw something like fire; and there was a radiance around Him.

As the appearance of the rainbow in the clouds on a rainy day, so was the appearance of the surrounding radiance. Such was the appearance of the likeness of the glory of the LORD. And when I saw it, I fell on my face and heard a voice speaking. (EZEKIEL 1:4–28 NASB)

God called Ezekiel with a vision of heaven, just as he did for the prophet Isaiah. Some scholars believe that the wheels within wheels represent God's power and direction. He is the one who directs the living creatures in their activities.

———— · ◈ · ————

In my vision, the man brought me back to the entrance of the Temple. There I saw a stream flowing east from beneath the door of the Temple and passing to the right of the altar on its south side. The man brought me outside the wall through the north gateway and led me around to the eastern entrance. There I could see the water flowing out through the south side of the east gateway.

Measuring as he went, he took me along the stream for 1,750 feet and then led me across. The water was up to my ankles. He measured off another 1,750 feet and led me across again. This time the water was up to my knees. After another 1,750 feet, it was up to my waist. Then he measured another 1,750 feet, and the river was too deep to walk across. It was deep enough to swim in, but too deep to walk through.

He asked me, "Have you been watching, son of man?" Then he led me back along the riverbank. When I returned, I was surprised by the sight of many trees growing on both sides of the river. Then he said to me, "This river flows east through the desert into the valley of the Dead Sea. The waters of this stream will make the salty waters of the Dead Sea fresh and pure. There will be swarms of living things wherever the water of this river flows. Fish will abound in the Dead Sea, for its waters will become fresh. Life will flourish wherever this water flows. Fishermen will stand along the shores of the Dead Sea. All the way from En-gedi to En-eglaim, the shores will be covered with nets drying in the sun. Fish of every kind will fill the Dead Sea, just as they fill the Mediterranean. But the marshes and swamps will not be purified; they will still be salty. Fruit trees of all kinds will grow along both sides of the river. The leaves of these trees will never turn brown and fall, and there will always be fruit on their branches. There will be a new crop every month, for they are watered by the river flowing from the Temple. The fruit will be for food and the leaves for healing" (**EZEKIEL 47:1–12** NLT).

Scholars are not quite sure whether the temple Ezekiel tours will be an actual temple during Christ's millennial rule (Revelation 20:1–6) or a metaphor. Also, later in this chapter Ezekiel sees a vision of land allotments given to the tribes of Israel, including a city that may or may not be New Jerusalem in heaven (47:13–48:34).

———— ❖ ————

The secret was revealed to Daniel in a vision during the night. So Daniel praised the God of heaven. . . . "But there is a God in heaven who reveals secrets. He will tell King Nebuchadnezzar what is going to happen in the days to come. . . . Your Majesty, you are the greatest king. The God of heaven has given you a kingdom. He has given you power, strength, and honor. . . . At the time of those kings, the God of heaven will establish a kingdom that will never be destroyed. No other people will be permitted to rule it. It will smash all the other kingdoms and put an end to them. But it will be established forever" (**DANIEL 2:19, 28, 37, 44** GOD's WORD).

———— ❖ ————

All the inhabitants of the earth are counted as nothing, and He does what He wants with the army of heaven and the inhabitants of the earth. There is no one who can hold back His hand or say to Him, "What have You done?" (**DANIEL 4:35** HCSB).

I kept looking until thrones were set up, and the Ancient of Days took His seat; His vesture was like white snow and the hair of His head like pure wool. His throne was ablaze with flames, its wheels were a burning fire. A river of fire was flowing and coming out from before Him; thousands upon thousands were attending Him, and myriads upon myriads were standing before Him; the court sat, and the books were opened.

Then I kept looking because of the sound of the boastful words which the horn was speaking; I kept looking until the beast was slain, and its body was destroyed and given to the burning fire.

As for the rest of the beasts, their dominion was taken away, but an extension of life was granted to them for an appointed period of time.

I kept looking in the night visions, and behold, with the clouds of heaven one like a Son of Man was coming, and He came up to the Ancient of Days and was presented before Him. And to Him was given dominion, Glory and a kingdom, that all the peoples, nations and men of every language might serve Him. His dominion is an everlasting dominion which will not pass away; and His kingdom is one which will not be destroyed. **(DANIEL 7:9–14 NASB)**

Many of Daniel's visions directly or indirectly relate to heaven. Here Daniel sees God on his throne. Since God is spirit (John 4:24), most scholars think the things Daniel sees are probably symbolic. The hair like wool represents wisdom. His white clothes symbolize purity. Also Daniel, like the prophet Ezekiel (see Ezekiel 1 above), mentions wheels— again a symbol of God's power. The Ancient of Days gives dominion to the Son of Man, which is a name Jesus called himself. (See Matthew 8:20.)

At that time Michael, the archangel who stands guard over your nation, will arise. Then there will be a time of anguish greater than any since nations first came into existence. But at that time every one of your people whose name is written in the book will be rescued. Many of those whose bodies lie dead and buried will rise up, some to everlasting life and some to shame and everlasting disgrace. Those who are wise will shine as bright as the sky, and those who lead many to righteousness will shine like the stars forever. But you, Daniel, keep this prophecy a secret; seal up the book until the time of the end, when many will rush here and there, and knowledge will increase" (DANIEL 12:1–4 NLT).

Here Daniel describes the resurrection of believers during the end times. Michael the archangel—an angelic leader—is mentioned here and in chapter 10 of Daniel. Believers' names are recorded in "the book," which is the Book of Life discussed in Revelation 20:12–15.

Then you will know that I am the LORD your God, who dwells in Zion, My holy mountain. Jerusalem will be holy, and foreigners will never overrun it again. In that day the mountains will drip with sweet wine, and the hills will flow with milk. All the streams of Judah will flow with water, and a spring will issue from the LORD's house, watering the Valley of Acacias. Egypt will become desolate, and Edom a desert wasteland, because of the violence [done] to the people of Judah in whose land they shed innocent blood. But Judah will be inhabited forever, and Jerusalem from generation to generation. I will pardon their bloodguilt, [which] I have not pardoned, for the LORD dwells in Zion. (JOEL 3:17–21 HCSB)

Here Joel provides an interlude of hope after a prophecy of judgment. Although God restored the people of Judah to their land after the exile, this prophecy points to a time of great peace—either the millennial kingdom of the Messiah or heaven.

"In that day I will restore the fallen house of David. I will repair its damaged walls. From the ruins I will rebuild it and restore its former glory. And Israel will possess what is left of Edom and all the nations I have called to be mine." The Lord has spoken, and he will do these things.

"The time will come," says the Lord, "when the grain and grapes will grow faster than they can be harvested. Then the terraced vineyards on the hills of Israel will drip with sweet wine! I will bring my exiled people of Israel back from distant lands, and they will rebuild their ruined cities and live in them again. They will plant vineyards and gardens; they will eat their crops and drink their wine. I will firmly plant them there in their own land. They will never again be uprooted from the land I have given them," says the Lord your God. **(AMOS 9:11–15 NLT)**

This promise of restoration has not happened yet, but it refers to either the millennial rule of Christ or heaven.

Then those of the Negev will possess the mountain of Esau, and those of the Shephelah the Philistine plain; also, they will possess the territory of Ephraim and the territory of Samaria, and Benjamin will possess Gilead. And the exiles of this host of the sons of Israel, who are among the Canaanites as far as Zarephath, and the exiles of Jerusalem who are in Sepharad will possess the cities of the Negev. The deliverers will ascend Mount Zion to judge the mountain of Esau, and the kingdom will be the LORD's. **(OBADIAH 19–21 NASB)**

This portrait of a restored Judah will take place in the future; again, perhaps this is the millennial kingdom of Christ or heaven.

———— • ◆ • ————

"Then I will purify the lips of the peoples, that all of them may call on the name of the LORD and serve him shoulder to shoulder. From beyond the rivers of Cush my worshipers, my scattered people, will bring me offerings. On that day you, Jerusalem, will not be put to shame for all the wrongs you have done to me, because I will remove from you your arrogant boasters. Never again will you be haughty on my holy hill. But I will leave within you the meek and humble. The remnant of Israel will trust in the name of the LORD.

"They will do no wrong; they will tell no lies. A deceitful tongue will not be found in their mouths. They will eat and lie down and no one will make them afraid.

"Sing, Daughter Zion; shout aloud, Israel! Be glad and rejoice with all your heart, Daughter Jerusalem! The LORD has taken away your punishment, he has turned back your enemy. The LORD, the King of Israel, is with you; never again will you fear any harm. On that day they will say to Jerusalem, "Do not fear, Zion; do not let your hands hang limp.

"The LORD your God is with you, the Mighty Warrior who saves. He will take great delight in you; in his love he will no longer rebuke you, but will rejoice over you with singing.

"I will remove from you all who mourn over the loss of your appointed festivals, which is a burden and reproach for you. At that time I will deal with all who oppressed you. I will rescue the lame; I will gather the exiles. I will give them praise and honor in every land where they have suffered shame. At that time I will gather you; at that time I will bring you home. I will give you honor and praise among all the peoples of the earth when I restore your fortunes before your very eyes," says the LORD. **(ZEPHANIAH 3:9–20 NIV)**

> *This passage provides another picture of the ultimate restoration to come in what is probably the millennial reign of Christ. Zephaniah describes the purity of language and worship and the lack of sin or fear among God's people.*

———— ❖ ————

The LORD's day of judging is coming when the wealth you have taken will be divided among you. I will bring all the nations together to fight Jerusalem. They will capture the city and rob the houses and attack the women. Half the people will be taken away as captives, but the rest of the people won't be taken from the city.

Then the LORD will go to war against those nations; he will fight as in a day of battle. On that day he will stand on the Mount of Olives, east of Jerusalem. The Mount of Olives will split in two, forming a deep valley that runs east and west. Half the mountain will move toward the north, and half will move toward the south. You will run through this mountain valley to the other side, just as you ran from the earthquake when Uzziah was king of Judah. Then the LORD my God will come and all the holy ones with him.

On that day there will be no light, cold, or frost. There will be no other day like it, and the LORD knows when it will come. There will be no day or night; even at evening it will still be light.

At that time fresh water will flow from Jerusalem. Half

of it will flow east to the Dead Sea, and half will flow west to the Mediterranean Sea. It will flow summer and winter.

Then the LORD will be king over the whole world. At that time there will be only one LORD, and his name will be the only name.

All the land south of Jerusalem from Geba to Rimmon will be turned into a plain. Jerusalem will be raised up, but it will stay in the same place. The city will reach from the Benjamin Gate and to the First Gate to the Corner Gate, and from the Tower of Hananel to the king's winepresses. People will live there, and it will never be destroyed again. Jerusalem will be safe.

But the LORD will bring a terrible disease on the nations that fought against Jerusalem. Their flesh will rot away while they are still standing up. Their eyes will rot in their sockets, and their tongues will rot in their mouths. At that time the LORD will cause panic. Everybody will grab his neighbor, and they will attack each other. The people of Judah will fight in Jerusalem. And the wealth of the nations around them will be collected—much gold, silver, and clothes. A similar disease will strike the horses, mules, camels, donkeys, and all the animals in the camps.

All of those left alive of the people who came to fight Jerusalem will come back to Jerusalem year after year to worship the King, the LORD All-Powerful, and to celebrate the Feast of Shelters. Anyone from the nations who does not go to Jerusalem to worship the King, the LORD All-Powerful, will not have rain fall on his land. If the Egyptians do not go to Jerusalem, they will not have rain. Then the LORD will send them the same terrible disease he sent the other nations that did not celebrate the Feast of Shelters. This will be the punishment for Egypt and any nation which does not go to celebrate the Feast of Shelters.

At that time the horses' bells will have written on them: HOLY TO THE LORD. The cooking pots in the Temple of the LORD will be like the holy altar bowls. Every pot in Jerusalem and Judah will be holy to the LORD All-Powerful, and everyone who offers sacrifices will be able to take food from them and cook in them. At that time there will not be any buyers or sellers in the Temple of the LORD All-Powerful. **(ZECHARIAH 14 NCV)**

The prophet Zechariah predicts the final judgment (the day of the LORD) and mentions the future rule of Christ.

————— ⚬ ⬥ ⚬ —————

"For behold, the day is coming, burning like an oven, and all the proud, yes, all who do wickedly will be stubble. And the day which is coming shall burn them up," says the LORD of hosts, "That will leave them neither root nor branch. But to you who fear My name the Sun of Righteousness shall arise with healing in His wings; and you shall go out and grow fat like stall-fed calves" **(MALACHI 4:1–2 NKJV)**.

The prophet Malachi, the last prophet in the Old Testament, predicts the coming judgment, just as other Old Testament prophets have done. Scholars believe that the "Sun of Righteousness" is Christ, who rewards the faithful in heaven.

CHAPTER 2

Many Mansions: New Testament Visions of Heaven

The glory of Him who moveth everything
Doth penetrate the universe, and shine
In one part more and in another less.
Within that heaven which most his light receives
Was I, and things beheld which to repeat
Nor knows, nor can, who from above descends;
Because in drawing near to its desire
Our intellect ingulphs itself so far,
That after it the memory cannot go.

—Dante Alighieri, *The Divine Comedy*[2]

Introduction

When the humble son of the carpenter Joseph came on the scene in first-century Jerusalem, heaven became more than just a distant realm occupied by God, his angels, and Jewish believers who died. Thanks to the sacrificial death and resurrection of Jesus, heaven became a real destination to which anyone—even Gentiles—could book a ticket. The price of admission has already been paid for by the king of the realm, who has nail-scarred hands. This king, the long-awaited

Messiah and Son of God, has promised to prepare a place for those who trust him to lead them there.

Be glad *and* supremely joyful, for your reward in heaven is great (strong and intense), for in this same way people persecuted the prophets who were before you. (**MATTHEW 5:12** AMP)

This verse is from Jesus' Sermon on the Mount in Matthew's gospel. Those who remain firm through persecution will be rewarded in heaven.

But I say unto you, Swear not at all; neither by heaven; for it is God's throne. (**MATTHEW 5:34** KJV)

The law of Moses was very clear on the subject of vows (Numbers 30). If you made a vow, you had to keep it. Even more important than vows was the name of God, and heaven is an extension of that.

So when you pray, you should pray like this: Our Father in heaven, may your name always be kept holy. May your kingdom come and what you want be done, here on earth as it is in heaven. (**MATTHEW 6:9–10** NCV)

Do not store up for yourselves treasures on earth, where moths and vermin destroy, and where thieves break in and steal. But store up for yourselves treasures in heaven, where moths and vermin do not destroy, and where thieves do not break in and steal. For where your treasure is, there your heart will be also. (MATTHEW 6:19–21 NIV)

———•◆•———

Sell your possessions and give to the poor. Make money-bags for yourselves that won't grow old, an inexhaustible treasure in heaven, where no thief comes near and no moth destroys. For where your treasure is, there your heart will be also. (LUKE 12:33–34 HCSB)

———•◆•———

Jesus replied, "The Son of Man is the farmer who plants the good seed. The field is the world, and the good seed represents the people of the Kingdom. The weeds are the people who belong to the evil one. The enemy who planted the weeds among the wheat is the devil. The harvest is the end of the world, and the harvesters are the angels.

"Just as the weeds are sorted out and burned in the fire, so it will be at the end of the world. The Son of Man will send his angels, and they will remove from his Kingdom everything that causes sin and all who do evil. And the angels will throw them into the fiery furnace, where there will be weeping and gnashing of teeth. Then the righteous will shine like the sun in their Father's Kingdom. Anyone with ears to hear should listen and understand!" (MATTHEW 13:37–43 NLT).

Jesus explains the parable of the weeds (Matthew 13:24–30). Here "the Kingdom" refers to heaven, a place where there will be no sin or evil.

———•◆•———

Jesus replied, "Simon, son of Jonah, you are blessed! No human revealed this to you, but my Father in heaven revealed it to you. You are Peter, and I can guarantee that on this rock I will build my church. And the gates of hell will not overpower it. I will give you the keys of the kingdom of heaven. Whatever you imprison, God will imprison. And whatever you set free, God will set free" (MATTHEW 16:17–19 GOD'S WORD).

Jesus responds to Peter's confession that Jesus is the Son of God (v. 16). The "keys of the kingdom" may refer to the God-given authority to preach the gospel. Heaven is "unlocked" only through Jesus—the only way to heaven (John 14:6). This authority is also shown in "imprisoning and setting free" ("binding and loosing" in other translations).

At that time the disciples came to Jesus, saying, "Who is the greatest in the kingdom of heaven?"

And calling to him a child, he put him in the midst of them and said, "Truly, I say to you, unless you turn and become like children, you will never enter the kingdom of heaven. Whoever humbles himself like this child is the greatest in the kingdom of heaven" (MATTHEW 18:1–4 ESV).

Be careful. Don't think these little children are worth nothing. I tell you that they have angels in heaven who are always with my Father in heaven. (MATTHEW 18:10 NCV)

Some scholars believe that the word angels *here refers to believers after death who "will see God" (Matthew 5:8), while others believe that the passage refers to literal angels. However, some make a case against the belief that every believer has a specific guardian angel. God might use any angel for any purpose.*

I assure you: Whatever you bind on earth is already bound in heaven, and whatever you loose on earth is already loosed in heaven. Again, I assure you: If two of you on earth agree about any matter that you pray for, it will be done for you by My Father in heaven.

For where two or three are gathered together in My name, I am there among them. **(MATTHEW 18:18–20 HCSB)**

> *When God-directed church discipline is implemented on earth, Jesus promises that heaven is in agreement. This action has the seal of approval from God.*

But do not be called Rabbi; for One is your Teacher, and you are all brothers. Do not call anyone on earth your father; for One is your Father, He who is in heaven. . . .

But woe to you, scribes and Pharisees, hypocrites, because you shut off the kingdom of heaven from people; for you do not enter in yourselves, nor do you allow those who are entering to go in. **(MATTHEW 23:8–9, 13 NASB)**

> *Jesus condemned the Pharisees and other leaders for thinking they were better than others and because they did not teach correctly about heaven.*

"Now learn the parable from the fig tree: when its branch has already become tender and puts forth its leaves, you know that summer is near; so, you too, when you see all these things, recognize that He is near, right at the door. Truly I say to you, this generation will not pass away until all these things take place. Heaven and earth will pass away, but My words will not pass away. But of that day and hour no one knows, not even the angels of heaven, nor the Son, but the Father alone.

"For the coming of the Son of Man will be just like the days of Noah. For as in those days before the flood they were eating and drinking, marrying and giving in marriage, until the day that Noah entered the ark, and they did not understand until the flood came and took them all away; so will the coming of the Son of Man be.

"Then there will be two men in the field; one will be taken and one will be left. Two women will be grinding at the mill; one will be taken and one will be left. Therefore be on the alert, for you do not know which day your Lord is coming. But be sure of this, that if the head of the house had known at what time of the night the thief was coming, he would have been on the alert and would not have allowed his house to be broken into.

"For this reason you also must be ready; for the Son of Man is coming at an hour when you do not think He will" **(MATTHEW 24:32–44 NASB).**

Jesus saith unto him, Thou hast said: nevertheless I say unto you, Hereafter shall ye see the Son of man sitting on the right hand of power, and coming in the clouds of heaven. **(MATTHEW 26:64 KJV)**

And Jesus came and said to them, "All authority in heaven and on earth has been given to me" **(MATTHEW 28:18 ESV).**

After Jesus' sacrificial death and resurrection, Jesus now claims the authority given to him by the Father—absolute authority over all of heaven and earth.

———— ◈ ————

And when He came up out of the water, at once he [John] saw the heavens torn open and the [Holy] Spirit like a dove coming down [to enter] into Him. And there came a voice out from within heaven, You are My Beloved Son; in You I am well pleased. (MARK 1:10–11 AMP)

This takes place during Jesus' baptism by John.

———— ◈ ————

What blessings await you when people hate you and exclude you and mock you and curse you as evil because you follow the Son of Man. When that happens, be happy! Yes, leap for joy! For a great reward awaits you in heaven. And remember, their ancestors treated the ancient prophets that same way. (LUKE 6:22–23 NLT)

———— ◈ ————

And he said unto them, I beheld Satan as lightning fall from heaven. (LUKE 10:18 KJV)

This statement of Jesus could either mean that he saw the actual event of Satan's fall or that Satan's fall has come about due to the coming of the Savior who has come to crush the serpent's heel (Genesis 3:15).

———— ◈ ————

"Nevertheless do not rejoice in this, that the spirits are subject to you, but rejoice that your names are recorded in heaven." At that very time He rejoiced greatly in the Holy Spirit, and said, "I praise You, O Father, Lord of heaven and earth, that You have hidden these things from the wise and intelligent and have revealed them to infants. Yes, Father, for this way was well-pleasing in Your sight" **(LUKE 10:20–21 NASB)**.

Jesus is speaking to the disciples, who were able to cast out demons in Jesus' name.

Others tested him by asking for a sign from heaven. **(LUKE 11:16 NIV)**

A "sign from heaven" is a sign that Jesus is the Messiah.

Just so, I tell you, there will be more joy in heaven over one sinner who repents than over ninety-nine righteous persons who need no repentance. **(LUKE 15:7 ESV)**

Here's the lesson: Use your worldly resources to benefit others and make friends. Then, when your earthly possessions are gone, they will welcome you to an eternal home. **(LUKE 16:9 NLT)**

This piece of advice comes from Jesus' parable of the shrewd manager. Generous believers who share rather than hoard have the promise of an eternal reward.

And he said to him, "Truly, truly, I say to you, you will see heaven opened, and the angels of God ascending and descending on the Son of Man" **(JOHN 1:51 ESV)**.

Jesus' words are an allusion to Jacob's vision in Genesis 28:10–19 (see chapter 5). As the promised Messiah, he is the new Jacob with authority over angels, who travel between heaven and earth.

———•◆•———

No one has gone to heaven except the Son of Man, who came from heaven. (JOHN 3:13 GOD'S WORD)

———•◆•———

The Jews then murmured at him, because he said, "I am the bread which came down from heaven." And they said, "Is not this Jesus, the son of Joseph, whose father and mother we know? how is it then that he saith, I came down from heaven?"

Jesus therefore answered and said unto them, "Murmur not among yourselves. No man can come to me, except the Father which hath sent me draw him: and I will raise him up at the last day. It is written in the prophets, And they shall be all taught of God. Every man therefore that hath heard, and hath learned of the Father, cometh unto me.

"Not that any man hath seen the Father, save he which is of God, he hath seen the Father. Verily, verily, I say unto you, He that believeth on me hath everlasting life. I am that bread of life. Your fathers did eat manna in the wilderness, and are dead. This is the bread which cometh down from heaven, that a man may eat thereof, and not die.

"I am the living bread which came down from heaven: if any man eat of this bread, he shall live for ever: and the bread that I will give is my flesh, which I will give for the life of the world."

The Jews therefore strove among themselves, saying, "How can this man give us his flesh to eat?"

Then Jesus said unto them, "Verily, verily, I say unto you, Except ye eat the flesh of the Son of man, and drink his blood, ye have no life in you. Whoso eateth my flesh, and drinketh my blood, hath eternal life; and I will raise him up at the last day. For my flesh is meat indeed, and my blood is drink indeed. He that eateth my flesh, and drinketh my blood, dwelleth in me, and I in him. As the living Father hath sent me, and I live by the Father: so he that eateth me, even he shall live by me. This is that bread which came down from heaven: not as your fathers did eat manna, and are dead: he that eateth of this bread shall live for ever" (JOHN 6:41–58 KJV).

"Don't be troubled. Believe in God, and believe in me. My Father's house has many rooms. If that were not true, would I have told you that I'm going to prepare a place for you? If I go to prepare a place for you, I will come again. Then I will bring you into my presence so that you will be where I am. You know the way to the place where I am going."

Thomas said to him, "Lord, we don't know where you're going. So how can we know the way?"

Jesus answered him, "I am the way, the truth, and the life. No one goes to the Father except through me. If you have known me, you will also know my Father. From now on you know him through me and have seen him in me" (JOHN 14:1–7 GOD'S WORD).

Heaven is my throne, and the earth is my footstool. What kind of house will you build for me, says the Lord, or what is the place of my rest? (ACTS 7:49 ESV)

When they heard these things, they were enraged in their hearts and gnashed their teeth at him. But Stephen, filled by the Holy Spirit, gazed into heaven. He saw God's glory, with Jesus standing at the right hand of God, and he said, "Look! I see the heavens opened and the Son of Man standing at the right hand of God!" (ACTS 7:54–56 HCSB).

Just before he is killed for his faith in Jesus, God grants Stephen a vision of Jesus in heaven, standing to receive him. In most quotations involving Jesus at the right hand of the Father, he is seated. Here, he stands.

For I consider that the sufferings of this present time are not worth comparing with the glory that is to be revealed to us. For the creation waits with eager longing for the revealing of the sons of God. For the creation was subjected to futility, not willingly, but because of him who subjected it, in hope that the creation itself will be set free from its bondage to corruption and obtain the freedom of the glory of the children of God. For we know that the whole creation has been groaning together in the pains of childbirth until now. And not only the creation, but we ourselves, who have the firstfruits of the Spirit, groan inwardly as we wait eagerly for adoption as sons, the redemption of our bodies. For in this hope we were saved. Now hope that is seen is not hope. For who hopes for what he sees? But if we hope for what we do not see, we wait for it with patience. . . .

No, in all these things we are more than conquerors through him who loved us. For I am sure that neither death nor life, nor angels nor rulers, nor things present nor things to come, nor powers, nor height nor depth, nor anything else in all creation, will be able to separate us from the love of God in Christ Jesus our Lord. (ROMANS 8:18–25, 37–39 ESV)

For we know in part and we prophesy in part, but when the perfect comes, the partial will pass away. . . . For now we see in a mirror dimly, but then face to face. Now I know in part; then I shall know fully, even as I have been fully known. **(1 CORINTHIANS 13:9–10, 12 ESV)**

> *Here Paul looks forward to the return of Jesus and how some mysteries will be cleared up in heaven.*

————— • ◈ • —————

But someone will ask, "How are the dead raised? With what kind of body will they come?" How foolish! What you sow does not come to life unless it dies. When you sow, you do not plant the body that will be, but just a seed, perhaps of wheat or of something else. But God gives it a body as he has determined, and to each kind of seed he gives its own body. Not all flesh is the same: People have one kind of flesh, animals have another, birds another and fish another. There are also heavenly bodies and there are earthly bodies; but the splendor of the heavenly bodies is one kind, and the splendor of the earthly bodies is another. The sun has one kind of splendor, the moon another and the stars another; and star differs from star in splendor.

So will it be with the resurrection of the dead. The body that is sown is perishable, it is raised imperishable; it is sown in dishonor, it is raised in glory; it is sown in weakness, it is raised in power; it is sown a natural body, it is raised a spiritual body.

If there is a natural body, there is also a spiritual body. So it is written: "The first man Adam became a living being"; the last Adam, a life-giving spirit. The spiritual did not come first, but the natural, and after that the spiritual. The first man was of the dust of the earth; the second man is of heaven. As was the earthly man, so are those who are of the earth; and as is the heavenly man, so also are those who are of heaven. And just as we have borne the image of the earthly man, so shall we bear the image of the heavenly man.

I declare to you, brothers and sisters, that flesh and blood cannot inherit the kingdom of God, nor does the perishable inherit the imperishable. Listen, I tell you a mystery: We will not all sleep, but we will all be changed—in a flash, in the twinkling of an eye, at the last trumpet. For the trumpet will sound, the dead will be raised imperishable, and we will be changed. For the perishable must clothe itself with the imperishable, and the mortal with immortality. When the perishable has been clothed with the imperishable, and the mortal with immortality, then the saying that is written will come true: "Death has been swallowed up in victory."

"Where, O death, is your victory? Where, O death, is your sting?"

The sting of death is sin, and the power of sin is the law. But thanks be to God! He gives us the victory through our Lord Jesus Christ. **(1 CORINTHIANS 15:35–57 NIV)**

For we know that if our earthly house, this tent, is destroyed, we have a building from God, a house not made with hands, eternal in the heavens. **(2 CORINTHIANS 5:1 NKJV)**

But the Jerusalem above is free, and she is our mother. **(GALATIANS 4:26 ESV)**

In contrasting the children of Hagar (v. 25) with the children of Sarah (v. 28), Paul refers to the Jerusalem in heaven (see Revelation 21:2) as prophesied by Isaiah (Isaiah 54:1). The children of Hagar represent salvation through works while the children of Sarah represent salvation through faith.

―――――◦―◆―◦―――――

Therefore God has highly exalted him and bestowed on him the name that is above every name, so that at the name of Jesus every knee should bow, in heaven and on earth and under the earth, and every tongue confess that Jesus Christ is Lord, to the glory of God the Father. **(PHILIPPIANS 2:9–11 ESV)**

―――――◦―◆―◦―――――

For our citizenship is in heaven, from which also we eagerly wait for a Savior, the Lord Jesus Christ; who will transform the body of our humble state into conformity with the body of His glory, by the exertion of the power that He has even to subject all things to Himself. **(PHILIPPIANS 3:20–21 NASB)**

Those trusting in Christ as Savior no longer belong to the earth. Therefore, they should act like citizens of heaven.

―――――◦―◆―◦―――――

We always thank God, the Father of our Lord Jesus Christ, when we pray for you, because we have heard of your faith in Christ Jesus and of the love you have for all God's people— the faith and love that spring from the hope stored up for you in heaven and about which you have already heard in the true message of the gospel that has come to you. In the same way, the gospel is bearing fruit and growing throughout the whole world—just as it has been doing among you since the day you heard it and truly understood God's grace. **(COLOSSIANS 1:3–6 NIV)**

―――――◦―◆―◦―――――

He created all things in heaven and on earth, visible and invisible. Whether they are kings or lords, rulers or powers—everything has been created through him and for him. **(COLOSSIANS 1:16 GOD'S WORD)**

> *Paul asserts that Jesus has authority because he was active in the creation of heaven and earth before he came to earth as a man.*

And to give relief to you who are afflicted and to us as well when the Lord Jesus will be revealed from heaven with His mighty angels in flaming fire, dealing out retribution to those who do not know God and to those who do not obey the gospel of our Lord Jesus. **(2 THESSALONIANS 1:7–8 NASB)**

> *When Jesus returns to earth from heaven, he will judge the disobedient. Believers, however, can anticipate Jesus' coming with relief and joy.*

He is the radiance of His glory, the exact expression of His nature, and He sustains all things by His powerful word. After making purification for sins, He sat down at the right hand of the Majesty on high. **(HEBREWS 1:3 HCSB)**

> *The New Testament view of God and other heavenly dwellers is that they have a shining radiance (glory). Jesus is a reflection of that glory. In other words, he is God.*

We need to hold on to our declaration of faith: We have a superior chief priest who has gone through the heavens. That person is Jesus, the Son of God. We have a chief priest who is

45

able to sympathize with our weaknesses. He was tempted in every way that we are, but he didn't sin. So we can go confidently to the throne of God's kindness to receive mercy and find kindness, which will help us at the right time. **(HEBREWS 4:14–16 GOD'S WORD)**

> *The people of Israel believed that there was more than one level of heaven, hence the word* heavens *here. The Talmud mentions seven levels. Paul talked of a third heaven (2 Corinthians 12:2).*

Abraham was confidently looking forward to a city with eternal foundations, a city designed and built by God.... All these people died still believing what God had promised them. They did not receive what was promised, but they saw it all from a distance and welcomed it. They agreed that they were foreigners and nomads here on earth. Obviously people who say such things are looking forward to a country they can call their own. If they had longed for the country they came from, they could have gone back. But they were looking for a better place, a heavenly homeland. That is why God is not ashamed to be called their God, for he has prepared a city for them. **(HEBREWS 11:10, 13–16 NLT)**

Therefore, since we are surrounded by such a great cloud of witnesses, let us throw off everything that hinders and the sin that so easily entangles, and let us run with perseverance the race marked out for us. Let us fix our eyes on Jesus, the author and perfecter of our faith, who for the joy set before him endured the cross, scorning its shame, and sat down at the right hand of the throne of God. **(HEBREWS 12:1–2 NIV)**

The writer of Hebrews talks of those in heaven who watch the actions of believers on earth. Having already run the race, these believers act as spectators for the contestants left in the race.

But you have come to Mount Zion, to the city of the living God, the heavenly Jerusalem. You have come to thousands upon thousands of angels in joyful assembly, to the church of the firstborn, whose names are written in heaven. You have come to God, the Judge of all, to the spirits of the righteous made perfect, to Jesus the mediator of a new covenant, and to the sprinkled blood that speaks a better word than the blood of Abel. **(HEBREWS 12:22–24 NIV)**

Let us then go to Him outside the camp, bearing His disgrace. For here we do not have an enduring city; instead, we seek the one to come. **(HEBREWS 13:13–14 HCSB)**

This passage is an admonition to endure suffering, just as Christ endured suffering. The "enduring city" is the New Jerusalem—the shining city in heaven which will last eternally, unlike the cities on earth.

Now we hope for the blessings God has for his children. These blessings, which cannot be destroyed or be spoiled or lose their beauty, are kept in heaven for you. **(1 PETER 1:4 NCV)**

It was shown them that their service was not for themselves but for you, when they told about the truths you have now heard. Those who preached the Good News to you told you those things with the help of the Holy Spirit who was sent from heaven—things into which angels desire to look. **(1 PETER 1:12 NCV)**

As Jesus explained, angels in heaven rejoice when a sinner repents (Luke 15:10). Here, Peter explains that angels are interested in the working out of salvation in the average believer.

Christ has gone to heaven where he has the highest position that God gives. Angels, rulers, and powers have been placed under his authority. **(1 PETER 3:22 GOD'S WORD)**

We [actually] heard this voice borne out of heaven, for we were together with Him on the holy mountain. **(2 PETER 1:18 AMP)**

Peter was present at Jesus' transfiguration (Matthew 17; see chapter 5) and heard the voice of God speaking of his Son, Jesus. He saw the heavenly glory Jesus bore and the Old Testament prophets—Moses and Elijah—alive again.

But the day of the Lord will come like a thief, and then the heavens will pass away with a roar, and the heavenly bodies will be burned up and dissolved, and the earth and the works that are done on it will be exposed.

Since all these things are thus to be dissolved, what sort of people ought you to be in lives of holiness and godliness, waiting for and hastening the coming of the day of God, because of which the heavens will be set on fire and dissolved, and the heavenly bodies will melt as they burn! But according to his promise we are waiting for new heavens and a new earth in which righteousness dwells. **(2 PETER 3:10–13** ESV**)**

⸻

Now to him who is able to keep you from stumbling and to present you blameless before the presence of his glory with great joy, to the only God, our Savior, through Jesus Christ our Lord, be glory, majesty, dominion, and authority, before all time and now and forever. Amen. **(JUDE 24–25** ESV**)**

CHAPTER 3

Heaven in the Book of Revelation

The talk that they had with the shining ones was about the glory of the place; who told them that the beauty and glory of it was inexpressible. There, said they, is "Mount Sion, the heavenly Jerusalem, the innumerable company of angels, and the spirits of just men made perfect. . . . You are going now, said they, to the paradise of God, wherein you shall see the tree of life, and eat of the never-fading fruits thereof.

—John Bunyan, *The Pilgrim's Progress*[3]

Introduction

There is no book of the Bible that talks about heaven more than the book of Revelation. Revelation falls under the category of "apocalyptic literature," which is a prophetic writing about the end times. The title itself comes from a Greek word *apokalypsis*, which means "disclosure, unveiling, revelation." Unlike the books of Daniel and Zechariah, which contain some apocalyptic writing, almost the whole book of Revelation is apocalyptic. Hidden truths about the upcoming time of judgment and the unveiling of New Jerusalem were revealed to the apostle John by the risen Christ through a series of visions—like "home movies" of heaven. These end times events inspired many writers centuries later, including John Bunyan, J. R. R. Tolkien, and C. S. Lewis. The visions recounted in Bunyan's masterwork, *The Pilgrim's Progress*, mirror the style of the apostle John's visions.

The emphasis in the book of Revelation is not on entertainment but enlightenment. The risen Christ had an urgent message, first to seven churches in Asia Minor (now Turkey). The seven churches—Ephesus, Smyrna, Pergamum, Thyatira, Sardis, Philadelphia, and Laodicea—were targets of false teachers. The Savior warned them and all believers throughout the world to be prepared for his coming.

Many of the images John saw while exiled on the island of Patmos were symbolic. Most were beyond description. Yet these frightening and glorious visions are the centerpiece of what heaven is really like: the place where everything reflects the glory of God; the place where "we shall see him as he is" (1 JOHN 3:2 ESV).

As with everything in the book of Revelation, numbers play a huge part. There are seven churches, seven seals, seven trumpets, seven bowls of wrath, twelve stars, etc. The number seven represents "completion," as does the number twelve.

Yet there are some in the church in Sardis who have not soiled their clothes with evil. They will walk with me in white, for they are worthy. All who are victorious will be clothed in white. I will never erase their names from the Book of Life, but I will announce before my Father and his angels that they are mine. Anyone with ears to hear must listen to the Spirit and understand what he is saying to the churches. (REVELATION 3:4–6 NLT)

I am coming soon. Hold on to what you have, so that no one will take away your crown. All who are victorious will become pillars in the Temple of my God, and they will never have to leave it. And I will write on them the name of my God, and they will be citizens in the city of my God—the new Jerusalem that comes down from heaven from my God. And I will also write on them my new name. **(REVELATION 3:11–12** NLT**)**

After these things I saw a door standing open in heaven. I heard the first voice like a trumpet speaking to me. It said, "Come up here, and I will show you what must happen after this."

Instantly, I came under the Spirit's power. I saw a throne in heaven, and someone was sitting on it.

The one sitting there looked like gray quartz and red quartz. There was a rainbow around the throne which looked like an emerald.

Around that throne were 24 other thrones, and on these thrones sat 24 leaders wearing white clothes. They had gold crowns on their heads. Lightning, noise, and thunder came from the throne. Seven flaming torches were burning in front of the throne. These are the seven spirits of God. In front of the throne, there was something like a sea of glass as clear as crystal. In the center near the throne and around the throne were four living creatures covered with eyes in front and in back. The first living creature was like a lion, the second was like a young bull, the third had a face like a human, and the fourth was like a flying eagle.

Each of the four living creatures had six wings and were covered with eyes, inside and out. Without stopping day or night they were singing, "Holy, holy, holy is the Lord God Almighty, who was, who is, and who is coming."

Whenever the living creatures give glory, honor, and thanks to the one who sits on the throne, to the one who lives forever and ever, the 24 leaders bow in front of the one who sits on the throne and worship the one who lives forever and ever. They place their crowns in front of the throne and say, "Our Lord and God, you deserve to receive glory, honor, and power because you created everything. Everything came into existence and was created because of your will" **(REVELATION 4 GOD's WORD)**.

Through the vision of heaven the Holy Spirit gives him, John sees the throne room of God. This is a symbol of God's authority and glory. The twenty-four elders are seen by scholars as a class of angelic being rather than as human rulers.

————— • ◆ • —————

And I saw in the right hand of Him who sat on the throne a scroll written inside and on the back, sealed with seven seals. Then I saw a strong angel proclaiming with a loud voice, "Who is worthy to open the scroll and to loose its seals?" And no one in heaven or on the earth or under the earth was able to open the scroll, or to look at it.

So I wept much, because no one was found worthy to open and read the scroll, or to look at it. But one of the elders said to me, "Do not weep. Behold, the Lion of the tribe of Judah, the Root of David, has prevailed to open the scroll and to loose its seven seals."

And I looked, and behold, in the midst of the throne and of the four living creatures, and in the midst of the elders, stood a Lamb as though it had been slain, having seven horns and seven eyes, which are the seven Spirits of God sent out into all the earth. Then He came and took the scroll out of the right hand of Him who sat on the throne.

Now when He had taken the scroll, the four living creatures and the twenty-four elders fell down before the Lamb, each having a harp, and golden bowls full of incense, which are the prayers of the saints. And they sang a new song, saying: "You are worthy to take the scroll, and to open its seals; for You were slain, and have redeemed us to God by Your blood out of every tribe and tongue and people and nation, and have made us kings and priests to our God; and we shall reign on the earth."

Then I looked, and I heard the voice of many angels around the throne, the living creatures, and the elders; and the number of them was ten thousand times ten thousand, and thousands of thousands, saying with a loud voice: "Worthy is the Lamb who was slain to receive power and riches and wisdom, and strength and honor and glory and blessing!"

And every creature which is in heaven and on the earth and under the earth and such as are in the sea, and all that are in them, I heard saying: "Blessing and honor and glory and power *be* to Him who sits on the throne, and to the Lamb, forever and ever!"

Then the four living creatures said, "Amen!" And the twenty-four elders fell down and worshiped Him who lives forever and ever. **(REVELATION 5 NKJV)**

The focus here is on the worship of the Lamb of God. The scroll with its double inscription is symbolic of God's covenant with man and the curses that will shortly befall the earth as a consequence of breaking the covenant, which we'll see in chapter 6.

After this I saw four angels standing at the four corners of the earth, holding back the four winds of the earth, that no wind might blow on earth or sea or against any tree. Then I saw another angel ascending from the rising of the sun, with the seal of the living God, and he called with a loud voice to the four angels who had been given power to harm earth and sea, saying, "Do not harm the earth or the sea or the trees, until we have sealed the servants of our God on their foreheads." And I heard the number of the sealed, 144,000, sealed from every tribe of the sons of Israel: 12,000 from the tribe of Judah were sealed, 12,000 from the tribe of Reuben, 12,000 from the tribe of Gad, 12,000 from the tribe of Asher, 12,000 from the tribe of Naphtali, 12,000 from the tribe of Manasseh, 12,000 from the tribe of Simeon, 12,000 from the tribe of Levi, 12,000 from the tribe of Issachar, 12,000 from the tribe of Zebulun, 12,000 from the tribe of Joseph, 12,000 from the tribe of Benjamin were sealed.

After this I looked, and behold, a great multitude that no one could number, from every nation, from all tribes and peoples and languages, standing before the throne and before the Lamb, clothed in white robes, with palm branches in their hands, and crying out with a loud voice, "Salvation belongs to our God who sits on the throne, and to the Lamb!" And all the angels were standing around the throne and around the elders and the four living creatures, and they fell on their faces before the throne and worshiped God, saying, "Amen! Blessing and glory and wisdom and thanksgiving and honor and power and might be to our God forever and ever! Amen."

Then one of the elders addressed me, saying, "Who are these, clothed in white robes, and from where have they come?" I said to him, "Sir, you know." And he said to me, "These are the ones coming out of the great tribulation. They have washed their robes and made them white in the blood of the Lamb.

"Therefore they are before the throne of God, and serve him day and night in his temple; and he who sits on the throne will shelter them with his presence.

They shall hunger no more, neither thirst anymore; the sun shall not strike them, nor any scorching heat.

For the Lamb in the midst of the throne will be their shepherd, and he will guide them to springs of living water, and God will wipe away every tear from their eyes" **(REVELATION 7 ESV).**

Between God's judgments on earth, John sees a vision of the sealed 144,000 from the nation of Israel who accept Jesus as Savior. Scholars aren't sure whether the number is symbolic or represents actual people. But this is a vision of a victorious people, as their white robes show.

When he opened the seventh seal, there was silence in heaven for about half an hour. **(REVELATION 8:1 GOD'S WORD)**

This is a "rest" between judgments. The silence in heaven shows the seriousness of the coming judgment.

And I saw another mighty angel come down from heaven, clothed with a cloud: and a rainbow was upon his head, and his face was as it were the sun, and his feet as pillars of fire:

And he had in his hand a little book open: and he set his right foot upon the sea, and his left foot on the earth,

And cried with a loud voice, as when a lion roareth: and when he had cried, seven thunders uttered their voices.

And when the seven thunders had uttered their voices, I was about to write: and I heard a voice from heaven saying unto me, Seal up those things which the seven thunders uttered, and write them not.

And the angel which I saw stand upon the sea and upon the earth lifted up his hand to heaven,

And sware by him that liveth for ever and ever, who created heaven, and the things that therein are, and the earth, and the things that therein are, and the sea, and the things which are therein, that there should be time no longer:

But in the days of the voice of the seventh angel, when he shall begin to sound, the mystery of God should be finished, as he hath declared to his servants the prophets. **(REVELATION 10:1–7** kjv**)**

Another "rest" between judgments, which shows God's patience and mercy.

The seventh angel then blew [his] trumpet, and there were mighty voices in heaven, shouting, The dominion (kingdom, sovereignty, rule) of the world has now come into the possession and become the kingdom of our Lord and of His Christ (the Messiah), and He shall reign forever and ever (for the eternities of the eternities)!

Then the twenty-four elders [of the heavenly Sanhedrin], who sit on their thrones before God, prostrated themselves before Him and worshiped, exclaiming, To You we give thanks, Lord God Omnipotent, [the One] Who is and [ever] was, for assuming the high sovereignty and the great power that are Yours and beginning to reign.

And the heathen (the nations) raged, but Your wrath (retribution, indignation) came, the time when the dead will be judged and Your servants the prophets and saints rewarded— and those who revere (fear) Your name, both low and high and small and great—and [the time] for destroying the corrupters of the earth.

Then the sanctuary of God in heaven was thrown open, and the ark of His covenant was seen standing inside in His sanctuary; and there were flashes of lightning, loud rumblings (blasts, mutterings), peals of thunder, an earthquake, and a terrific hailstorm. **(REVELATION 11:15–19 AMP)**

This passage gives the signal for the second coming of Christ. Some scholars believe that this section shows the worship during the millennial rule of Christ.

————— · ◆ · —————

A great sign appeared in heaven: a woman clothed with the sun, and the moon under her feet, and on her head a crown of twelve stars; and she was with child; and she cried out, being in labor and in pain to give birth.

Then another sign appeared in heaven: and behold, a great red dragon having seven heads and ten horns, and on his heads were seven diadems.

And his tail swept away a third of the stars of heaven and threw them to the earth. And the dragon stood before the woman who was about to give birth, so that when she gave birth he might devour her child.

And she gave birth to a son, a male child, who is to rule all the nations with a rod of iron; and her child was caught up to God and to His throne. Then the woman fled into the wilderness where she had a place prepared by God, so that there she would be nourished for one thousand two hundred and sixty days.

And there was war in heaven, Michael and his angels waging war with the dragon. The dragon and his angels waged war, and they were not strong enough, and there was no longer a place found for them in heaven. And the great dragon was thrown down, the serpent of old who is called the devil and Satan, who deceives the whole world; he was thrown down to the earth, and his angels were thrown down with him.

Then I heard a loud voice in heaven, saying, "Now the salvation, and the power, and the kingdom of our God and the authority of His Christ have come, for the accuser of our brethren has been thrown down, he who accuses them before our God day and night.

"And they overcame him because of the blood of the Lamb and because of the word of their testimony, and they did not love their life even when faced with death.

"For this reason, rejoice, O heavens and you who dwell in them. Woe to the earth and the sea, because the devil has come down to you, having great wrath, knowing that he has *only* a short time."

And when the dragon saw that he was thrown down to the earth, he persecuted the woman who gave birth to the male child. But the two wings of the great eagle were given to the woman, so that she could fly into the wilderness to her place, where she was nourished for a time and times and half a time, from the presence of the serpent.

And the serpent poured water like a river out of his mouth after the woman, so that he might cause her to be swept away with the flood. But the earth helped the woman, and the earth opened its mouth and drank up the river which the dragon poured out of his mouth. So the dragon was enraged with the woman, and went off to make war with the rest of her children, who keep the commandments of God and hold to the testimony of Jesus. **(REVELATION 12 NASB)**

Scholars believe the woman clothed with the sun, moon, and stars represents Israel;, the child represents Christ;, and the red dragon represents Satan. The woman's identity is confirmed by Genesis 37:9, which describes Joseph's dream of the sun, moon, and stars bowing down to him. These images are identified as Jacob and his family—Israel. Ezekiel 29:3 uses the great dragon metaphor to describe the pharaoh of Egypt and also, on a larger scale, Satan. The image of the dragon sweeping the stars out of the sky corresponds with an image in Daniel 8:10. While Daniel referred to a ruler of the Seleucid dynasty—Antiochus IV Epiphanes—the apostle John relates the image to Satan.

Some scholars believe that the angels' victory over the dragon could either be Satan's actual fall from heaven (see Isaiah 14:12–15 in chapter 1; 2 Peter 2:4 and Jude 6 in chapter 2) or a symbol of Jesus' victory at the cross (a major defeat for Satan).

Then I looked, and behold, the Lamb stood on Mount Zion, and with Him 144,000 [men] who had His name and His Father's name inscribed on their foreheads.

And I heard a voice from heaven like the sound of great waters and like the rumbling of mighty thunder; the voice I heard [seemed like the music] of harpists accompanying themselves on their harps.

And they sang a new song before the throne [of God] and before the four living creatures and before the elders [of the heavenly Sanhedrin]. No one could learn [to sing] that song except the 144,000 who had been ransomed (purchased, redeemed) from the earth.

These are they who have not defiled themselves by relations with women, for they are [pure as] virgins. These are they who follow the Lamb wherever He goes. These are they who have been ransomed (purchased, redeemed) from among men as the firstfruits for God and the Lamb.

No lie was found to be upon their lips, for they are blameless (spotless, untainted, without blemish) before the throne of God.

Then I saw another angel flying in midair, with an eternal Gospel (good news) to tell to the inhabitants of the earth, to every race and tribe and language and people.

And he cried with a mighty voice, Revere God and give Him glory (honor and praise in worship), for the hour of His judgment has arrived. Fall down before Him; pay Him homage *and* adoration *and* worship Him Who created heaven and earth, the sea and the springs (fountains) of water.

Then another angel, a second, followed, declaring, Fallen, fallen is Babylon the great! She who made all nations drink of the [maddening] wine of her passionate unchastity [idolatry].

Then another angel, a third, followed them, saying with a mighty voice, Whoever pays homage to the beast and his statue and permits the [beast's] stamp (mark, inscription) to be put on his forehead or on his hand, He too shall [have to] drink of the wine of God's indignation *and* wrath, poured undiluted into the cup of His anger; and he shall be tormented with fire and brimstone in the presence of the holy angels and in the presence of the Lamb.

And the smoke of their torment ascends forever and ever; and they have no respite (no pause, no intermission, no rest, no peace) day or night—these who pay homage to the beast and to his image and whoever receives the stamp of his name upon him.

Here [comes in a call for] the steadfastness of the saints [the patience, the endurance of the people of God], those who [habitually] keep God's commandments and [their] faith in Jesus.

Then I heard further [perceiving the distinct words of] a voice from heaven, saying, Write this: Blessed (happy, to be envied) are the dead from now on who die in the Lord! Yes, blessed (happy, to be envied indeed), says the Spirit, [in] that they may rest from their labors, for their works (deeds) do follow (attend, accompany) them!

Again I looked, and behold, [I saw] a white cloud, and sitting on the cloud One resembling a Son of Man, with a crown of gold on His head and a sharp scythe (sickle) in His hand.

And another angel came out of the temple sanctuary, calling with a mighty voice to Him Who was sitting upon the cloud, Put in Your scythe and reap, for the hour has arrived to gather the harvest, for the earth's crop is fully ripened.

So He Who was sitting upon the cloud swung His scythe (sickle) on the earth, and the earth's crop was harvested.

Then another angel came out of the temple [sanctuary] in heaven, and he also carried a sharp scythe (sickle).

And another angel came forth from the altar, [the angel] who has authority *and* power over fire, and he called with a loud cry to him who had the sharp scythe (sickle), Put forth your scythe and reap the fruitage of the vine of the earth, for its grapes are entirely ripe.

So the angel swung his scythe on the earth and stripped the grapes and gathered the vintage from the vines of the earth and cast it into the huge winepress of God's indignation and wrath.

And [the grapes in] the winepress were trodden outside the city, and blood poured from the winepress, [reaching] as high as horses' bridles, for a distance of 1,600 stadia (about 200 miles). (REVELATION 14 AMP)

Before the announcements of upcoming judgments and the actual judgment of the seven plagues (Revelation 15), the apostle John provides an interlude of praise by those who have been redeemed. The notation of 144,000 is probably not the actual number of people.

The harvests described after the praise interlude might be a reference to the harvest of believers and unbelievers described in Jesus' parable of the weeds (Matthew 13:30).

————— ◆ —————

Then I saw another sign in heaven, great and marvelous, seven angels who had seven plagues, which are the last, because in them the wrath of God is finished.

And I saw something like a sea of glass mixed with fire, and those who had been victorious over the beast and his image and the number of his name, standing on the sea of glass, holding harps of God.

And they sang the song of Moses, the bond-servant of God, and the song of the Lamb, saying, "Great and marvelous are Your works, O Lord God, the Almighty; righteous and true are Your ways, King of the nations! "Who will not fear, O Lord, and glorify Your name? For You alone are holy; for ALL THE NATIONS WILL COME AND WORSHIP BEFORE YOU, FOR YOUR RIGHTEOUS ACTS HAVE BEEN REVEALED."

After these things I looked, and the temple of the tabernacle of testimony in heaven was opened, and the seven angels who had the seven plagues came out of the temple, clothed in linen, clean *and* bright, and girded around their chests with golden sashes.

Then one of the four living creatures gave to the seven angels seven golden bowls full of the wrath of God, who lives forever and ever.

And the temple was filled with smoke from the glory of God and from His power; and no one was able to enter the temple until the seven plagues of the seven angels were finished. **(REVELATION 15:1–8 NASB)**

The vision of the Ancient of Days in Daniel 7:10 is similar to the description of 15:2 above: "A river of fire was flowing and coming out from before Him; thousands upon thousands were attending Him, and myriads upon myriads were standing before Him; the court sat, and the books were opened." The living creatures are the cherubim described in Ezekiel 1.

———— ◆ ————

After this I heard something like the loud voice of a vast multitude in heaven, saying: Hallelujah! Salvation, glory, and power belong to our God, because His judgments are true and righteous, because He has judged the notorious prostitute who corrupted the earth with her sexual immorality; and He has avenged the blood of His servants that was on her hands.

A second time they said: Hallelujah! Her smoke ascends forever and ever!

Then the 24 elders and the four living creatures fell down and worshiped God, who is seated on the throne, saying: Amen! Hallelujah!

A voice came from the throne, saying: Praise our God, all you His servants, you who fear Him, both small and great!

Then I heard something like the voice of a vast multitude, like the sound of cascading waters, and like the rumbling of loud thunder, saying: Hallelujah—because our Lord God, the Almighty, has begun to reign! Let us be glad, rejoice, and give Him glory, because the marriage of the Lamb has come, and His wife has prepared herself.

She was permitted to wear fine linen, bright and pure. For the fine linen represents the righteous acts of the saints.

Then he said to me, "Write: Blessed are those invited to the marriage feast of the Lamb!" He also said to me, "These words of God are true." Then I fell at his feet to worship him, but he said to me, "Don't do that! I am a fellow slave with you and your brothers who have the testimony about Jesus. Worship God, because the testimony about Jesus is the spirit of prophecy."

Then I saw heaven opened, and there was a white horse! Its rider is called Faithful and True, and in righteousness He judges and makes war. His eyes were like a fiery flame, and on His head were many crowns. He had a name written that no one knows except Himself. He wore a robe stained with blood, and His name is called the Word of God. The armies that were in heaven followed Him on white horses, wearing pure white linen. From His mouth came a sharp sword, so that with it He might strike the nations. He will shepherd them with an iron scepter. He will also trample the winepress of the fierce anger of God, the Almighty. And on His robe and on His thigh He has a name written: KING OF KINGS AND LORD OF LORDS.

Then I saw an angel standing in the sun, and he cried out in a loud voice, saying to all the birds flying in mid-heaven, "Come, gather together for the great supper of God, so that you may eat the flesh of kings, the flesh of commanders, the flesh of mighty men, the flesh of horses and of their riders, and the flesh of everyone, both free and slave, small and great."

Then I saw the beast, the kings of the earth, and their armies gathered together to wage war against the rider on the horse and against His army. But the beast was taken prisoner, and along with him the false prophet, who had performed signs on his authority, by which he deceived those who accepted the mark of the beast and those who worshiped his image. Both of them were thrown alive into the lake of fire that burns with sulfur. The rest were killed with the sword that came from the mouth of the rider on the horse, and all the birds were filled with their flesh. (REVELATION 19 HCSB)

Here the final judgment of the nations and the Beast as promised by the prophets and Jesus (Ezekiel 38–39; Isaiah 49:3; 63:1–3; Matthew 13:40–42) takes place. Everyone in heaven rejoices as the Lamb, Jesus, begins his reign. As stated in Daniel 7:14, Jesus is given dominion over all. Like ancient kings before, he prepares the way of his reign by sweeping away his enemies: Satan and his angels, the Antichrist, and false prophet.

Then I saw an angel coming down from heaven, having the key to the bottomless pit and a great chain in his hand. He laid hold of the dragon, that serpent of old, who is the Devil and Satan, and bound him for a thousand years; and he cast him into the bottomless pit, and shut him up, and set a seal on him, so that he should deceive the nations no more till the thousand years were finished. But after these things he must be released for a little while.

And I saw thrones, and they sat on them, and judgment was committed to them. Then I saw the souls of those who had been beheaded for their witness to Jesus and for the word of God, who had not worshiped the beast or his image, and had not received *his* mark on their foreheads or on their hands. And they lived and reigned with Christ for a thousand years. But the rest of the dead did not live again until the thousand years were finished. This is the first resurrection. Blessed and holy *is* he who has part in the first resurrection. Over such the second death has no power, but they shall be priests of God and of Christ, and shall reign with Him a thousand years.

Now when the thousand years have expired, Satan will be released from his prison and will go out to deceive the nations which are in the four corners of the earth, Gog and Magog, to gather them together to battle, whose number is as the sand of the sea. They went up on the breadth of the earth and surrounded the camp of the saints and the beloved city. And fire came down from God out of heaven and devoured them. The devil, who deceived them, was cast into the lake of fire and brimstone where the beast and the false prophet are. And they will be tormented day and night forever and ever.

Then I saw a great white throne and Him who sat on it, from whose face the earth and the heaven fled away. And there was found no place for them. And I saw the dead, small and great, standing before God, and books were opened. And another book was opened, which is the Book of Life. And the dead were judged according to their works, by the things which were written in the books. The sea gave up the dead who were in it, and Death and Hades delivered up the dead who were in them. And they were judged, each one according to his works. Then Death and Hades were cast into the lake of fire. This is the second death. And anyone not found written in the Book of Life was cast into the lake of fire. **(REVELATION 20 NKJV)**

This chapter details the imprisonment and final destruction of Satan and his allies. Binding Satan most likely means that God will place limits on his power to harm others for one thousand years before his final destruction. Scholars debate whether this thousand years is literal or figurative.

Then I saw a new heaven and a new earth, for the first heaven and the first earth had passed away, and the sea was no more. And I saw the holy city, new Jerusalem, coming down out of heaven from God, prepared as a bride adorned for her husband. And I heard a loud voice from the throne saying, "Behold, the dwelling place of God is with man. He will dwell with them, and they will be his people, and God himself will be with them as their God. He will wipe away every tear from their eyes, and death shall be no more, neither shall there be mourning nor crying nor pain anymore, for the former things have passed away."

And he who was seated on the throne said, "Behold, I am making all things new." Also he said, "Write this down, for these words are trustworthy and true." And he said to me, "It is done! I am the Alpha and the Omega, the beginning and the end. To the thirsty I will give from the spring of the water of life without payment. The one who conquers will have this heritage, and I will be his God and he will be my son. But as for the cowardly, the faithless, the detestable, as for murderers, the sexually immoral, sorcerers, idolaters, and all liars, their portion will be in the lake that burns with fire and sulfur, which is the second death."

Then came one of the seven angels who had the seven bowls full of the seven last plagues and spoke to me, saying, "Come, I will show you the Bride, the wife of the Lamb." And he carried me away in the Spirit to a great, high mountain, and showed me the holy city Jerusalem coming down out of heaven from God, having the glory of God, its radiance like a most rare jewel, like a jasper, clear as crystal. It had a great, high wall, with twelve gates, and at the gates twelve angels, and on the gates the names of the twelve tribes of the sons of Israel were inscribed—on the east three gates, on the north three gates, on the south three gates, and on the west three gates. And the wall of the city had twelve foundations, and on them were the twelve names of the twelve apostles of the Lamb.

And the one who spoke with me had a measuring rod of gold to measure the city and its gates and walls. The city lies foursquare; its length the same as its width. And he measured the city with his rod, 12,000 stadia. Its length and width and height are equal. He also measured its wall, 144 cubits by human measurement, which is also an angel's measurement. The wall was built of jasper, while the city was pure gold, clear as glass. The foundations of the wall of the city were adorned with every kind of jewel. The first was jasper, the second sapphire, the third agate, the fourth emerald, the fifth onyx, the sixth carnelian, the seventh chrysolite, the eighth beryl, the ninth topaz, the tenth chrysoprase, the eleventh jacinth, the twelfth amethyst. And the twelve gates were twelve pearls, each of the gates made of a single pearl, and the street of the city was pure gold, transparent as glass.

And I saw no temple in the city, for its temple is the Lord God the Almighty and the Lamb. And the city has no need of sun or moon to shine on it, for the glory of God gives it light, and its lamp is the Lamb. By its light will the nations walk, and the kings of the earth will bring their glory into it, and its gates will never be shut by day—and there will be no night there. They will bring into it the glory and the honor of the nations. But nothing unclean will ever enter it, nor anyone who does what is detestable or false, but only those who are written in the Lamb's book of life. **(REVELATION 21 ESV)**

This chapter and chapter 22 are the crown jewels of Revelation—the hope of heaven many Old and New Testament writers described.

————— ◦ ◈ ◦ —————

Then the angel showed me the river of the water of life, as clear as crystal, flowing from the throne of God and of the Lamb down the middle of the great street of the city. On each side of the river stood the tree of life, bearing twelve crops of fruit, yielding its fruit every month. And the leaves of the tree are for the healing of the nations. No longer will there be any curse. The throne of God and of the Lamb will be in the city, and his servants will serve him. They will see his face, and his name will be on their foreheads. There will be no more night. They will not need the light of a lamp or the light of the sun, for the Lord God will give them light. And they will reign for ever and ever.

The angel said to me, "These words are trustworthy and true. The Lord, the God who inspires the prophets, sent his angel to show his servants the things that must soon take place."

"Look, I am coming soon! Blessed is the one who keeps the words of the prophecy written in this scroll."

I, John, am the one who heard and saw these things. And when I had heard and seen them, I fell down to worship at the feet of the angel who had been showing them to me. But he said to me, "Don't do that! I am a fellow servant with you and with your fellow prophets and with all who keep the words of this scroll. Worship God!"

Then he told me, "Do not seal up the words of the prophecy of this scroll, because the time is near. Let the one who does wrong continue to do wrong; let the vile person continue to be vile; let the one who does right continue to do right; and let the holy person continue to be holy."

"Look, I am coming soon! My reward is with me, and I will give to each person according to what they have done. I am the Alpha and the Omega, the First and the Last, the Beginning and the End.

"Blessed are those who wash their robes, that they may have the right to the tree of life and may go through the gates into the city. Outside are the dogs, those who practice magic arts, the sexually immoral, the murderers, the idolaters and everyone who loves and practices falsehood.

"I, Jesus, have sent my angel to give you this testimony

for the churches. I am the Root and the Offspring of David, and the bright Morning Star."

The Spirit and the bride say, "Come!" And let the one who hears say, "Come!" Let the one who is thirsty come; and let the one who wishes take the free gift of the water of life.

I warn everyone who hears the words of the prophecy of this scroll: If anyone adds anything to them, God will add to that person the plagues described in this scroll. And if anyone takes words away from this scroll of prophecy, God will take away from that person any share in the tree of life and in the Holy City, which are described in this scroll.

He who testifies to these things says, "Yes, I am coming soon." Amen. Come, Lord Jesus. The grace of the Lord Jesus be with God's people. Amen. **(REVELATION 22 NIV)**

CHAPTER 4

Between Heaven and Earth

Ah, why dost thou go on? Ah, why not stay?
Long since we all were slain by violence,
And sinners even to the latest hour;
Then did a light from heaven admonish us,
So that, both penitent and pardoning, forth
From life we issued reconciled to God,
Who with desire to see Him stirs our hearts.

—Dante Alighieri, *The Divine Comedy*[1]

Introduction

The pilot hears the crackle of the air traffic controller's voice bidding him or her to wait until the plane is allowed to head to the gate. A holding pattern is in effect. The wait is on.

Those who believed the prophecies of the coming of the Messiah long before Jesus died and rose again were in a holding pattern of sorts as they waited for the Messiah to come. Consequently, when they died, some believed they would be taken to a place known as Abraham's bosom—the place of paradise within Sheol (Hades).

Many today think that "holding place" is Purgatory, as the quote above suggests. Most Protestant Christians don't believe in Purgatory, but there are scriptural mysteries surrounding those places between heaven and earth. Some experiences on earth provide a taste of heaven, glimpses so potent, they color all of life. They are a stairway to a "far green country," a reminder that our world is just a waiting room for believers on the journey toward heaven. Yet for those who don't walk with Christ, these visions are a glimpse of judgment and a reminder that the God of heaven sees all.

When Enoch was 65 years old, he became the father of Methuselah. After he became the father of Methuselah, Enoch walked with God for 300 years and had other sons and daughters. Enoch lived a total of 365 years. Enoch walked with God; then he was gone because God took him. (**GENESIS 5:21–24 GOD'S WORD**)

Enoch is one of two individuals mentioned in the Bible who did not die. Instead, because of his blameless walk with God, he was mysteriously taken to be with God.

When the LORD was about to take Elijah up to heaven in a whirlwind, Elijah and Elisha were traveling from Gilgal. . . . As they were walking along and talking, suddenly a chariot of fire appeared, drawn by horses of fire. It drove between the two men, separating them, and Elijah was carried by a whirlwind into heaven. Elisha saw it and cried out, "My father! My father! I see the chariots and charioteers of Israel!" And as they disappeared from sight, Elisha tore his clothes in distress. (**2 KINGS 2:1, 11–12 NLT**)

Like Enoch, the prophet Elijah did not die. Instead he was taken directly to his eternal destination—with God.

———— • ❧ • ————

Jacob left Beersheba and set out for Haran. When he reached a certain place, he stopped for the night because the sun had set. Taking one of the stones there, he put it under his head and lay down to sleep. He had a dream in which he saw a stairway resting on the earth, with its top reaching to heaven, and the angels of God were ascending and descending on it. There above it stood the LORD, and he said: "I am the LORD, the God of your father Abraham and the God of Isaac. I will give you and your descendants the land on which you are lying. Your descendants will be like the dust of the earth, and you will spread out to the west and to the east, to the north and to the south. All peoples on earth will be blessed through you and your offspring. I am with you and will watch over you wherever you go, and I will bring you back to this land. I will not leave you until I have done what I have promised you."

When Jacob awoke from his sleep, he thought, "Surely the LORD is in this place, and I was not aware of it." He was afraid and said, "How awesome is this place! This is none other than the house of God; this is the gate of heaven."

Early the next morning Jacob took the stone he had placed under his head and set it up as a pillar and poured oil on top of it. He called that place Bethel, though the city used to be called Luz. **(GENESIS 28:10–19 NIV)**

Jacob's vision shows heaven as a real destination, one from which angels descended to earth and ascended back again. When he awoke, he perceived that he was still in the presence of God. Scholars debate whether there are certain places where heaven is "closer" to earth.

There was a certain rich man who was clothed in purple and fine linen and fared sumptuously every day. But there was a certain beggar named Lazarus, full of sores, who was laid at his gate, desiring to be fed with the crumbs which fell from the rich man's table. Moreover the dogs came and licked his sores. So it was that the beggar died, and was carried by the angels to Abraham's bosom. The rich man also died and was buried. And being in torments in Hades, he lifted up his eyes and saw Abraham afar off, and Lazarus in his bosom.

Then he cried and said, "Father Abraham, have mercy on me, and send Lazarus that he may dip the tip of his finger in water and cool my tongue; for I am tormented in this flame." But Abraham said, "Son, remember that in your lifetime you received your good things, and likewise Lazarus evil things; but now he is comforted and you are tormented. And besides all this, between us and you there is a great gulf fixed, so that those who want to pass from here to you cannot, nor can those from there pass to us."

Then he said, "I beg you therefore, father, that you would send him to my father's house, for I have five brothers, that he may testify to them, lest they also come to this place of torment." Abraham said to him, "They have Moses and the prophets; let them hear them." And he said, "No, father Abraham; but if one goes to them from the dead, they will repent." But he said to him, "If they do not hear Moses and the prophets, neither will they be persuaded though one rise from the dead" **(LUKE 16:19–31** NKJV**)**.

While Jesus often spoke in parables, the Bible does not state that this story was a parable. Jesus spoke as if recounting a real event. Some believe that "Abraham's bosom" refers to a place of comfort in Sheol (Hades) where believers were separated from unbelievers, who were in a place of fiery torment.

Other scholars believe that Abraham's bosom refers to the fellowship of other believers in heaven. The idea of being taken to the bosom of a respected leader comes from a custom shown in John 13:23, where John reclines next to Jesus and leans against him. Being so close to a beloved leader is a mark of special favor.

For as Jonah was in the belly of the great fish for three days and three nights, so will the Son of Man be in the heart of the earth for three days and three nights. **(MATTHEW 12:40 NLT)**

The concept of Hades or hell comes from Gehenna, a Hebrew reference for the Valley of Ben Hinnom, a dump site and a place of idol worship near Jerusalem that became synonymous with hell (2 Kings 23:10; Matthew 18:6–9; 23:15). This is where some believe that Jesus went to rescue the souls of believers after his crucifixion.

David was looking into the future and speaking of the Messiah's resurrection. He was saying that God would not leave him among the dead or allow his body to rot in the grave. **(ACTS 2:31 NLT)**

Here Peter quotes Psalm 16 (see also chapter 1 in this book). Many Bible translations use "the grave" rather than "hell." See also 1 Peter 3:18–20 in chapter 5.

Then [the thief] said, "Jesus, remember me when you come into your kingdom."

Jesus answered him, "I tell you the truth, today you will be with me in paradise" (LUKE 23:42–43 NIV).

Paradise (paradeisos in the Greek) comes from a Persian word referring to the garden of Eden. It also refers to heaven.

This boasting will do no good, but I must go on. I will reluctantly tell about visions and revelations from the Lord. I was caught up to the third heaven fourteen years ago. Whether I was in my body or out of my body, I don't know—only God knows. Yes, only God knows whether I was in my body or outside my body. But I do know that I was caught up to paradise and heard things so astounding that they cannot be expressed in words, things no human is allowed to tell. (2 CORINTHIANS 12:1–4 NLT)

Paul's vision of heaven represents the views of Jewish scholars at the time. Rather than referring to the sky or outer space, Paul refers to a third layer beyond that—the actual heaven where God lives.

When David looked up and saw the angel of the LORD standing between earth and heaven, with his drawn sword in his hand stretched out over Jerusalem, David and the elders, clothed in sackcloth, fell down with their faces [to the ground]. (1 CHRONICLES 21:16 HCSB)

Some visions of heaven were not positive. After David sinned by taking a census of the population (see also 2 Samuel 24), God allowed David a frightening between-two-worlds glimpse of the punishment to come.

If I go up to the heavens, you are there; if I make my bed in the depths, you are there. **(PSALM 139:8 NIV)**

The "depths" is another word for hell in contrast to heaven.

And it came to pass in the sixth year, in the sixth month, on the fifth day of the month, as I sat in my house with the elders of Judah sitting before me, that the hand of the Lord GOD fell upon me there. Then I looked, and there was a likeness, like the appearance of fire—from the appearance of His waist and downward, fire; and from His waist and upward, like the appearance of brightness, like the color of amber. He stretched out the form of a hand, and took me by a lock of my hair; and the Spirit lifted me up between earth and heaven, and brought me in visions of God to Jerusalem, to the door of the north gate of the inner court, where the seat of the image of jealousy was, which provokes to jealousy. And behold, the glory of the God of Israel was there, like the vision that I saw in the plain. **(EZEKIEL 8:1–4 NKJV)**

The prophet Ezekiel's vision of the glory of God introduces the subject of idolatry in the temple.

In those days I, Daniel, was mourning for three full weeks. I didn't eat any rich food, no meat or wine entered my mouth, and I didn't put any oil [on my body] until the three weeks were over. On the twenty-fourth day of the first month, as I was standing on the bank of the great river, the Tigris, I looked up, and there was a man dressed in linen, with a belt of gold from Uphaz around his waist. His body was like topaz, his face like the brilliance of lightning, his eyes like flaming torches, his arms and feet like the gleam of polished bronze, and the sound of his words like the sound of a multitude.

Only I, Daniel, saw the vision. The men who were with me did not see it, but a great terror fell on them, and they ran and hid. I was left alone, looking at this great vision. No strength was left in me; my face grew deathly pale, and I was powerless. I heard the words he said, and when I heard them I fell into a deep sleep, with my face to the ground.

Suddenly, a hand touched me and raised me to my hands and knees. He said to me, "Daniel, you are a man treasured [by God]. Understand the words that I'm saying to you. Stand on your feet, for I have now been sent to you." After he said this to me, I stood trembling.

"Don't be afraid, Daniel," he said to me, "for from the first day that you purposed to understand and to humble yourself before your God, your prayers were heard. I have come because of your prayers. But the prince of the kingdom of Persia opposed me for 21 days. Then Michael, one of the chief princes, came to help me after I had been left there with the kings of Persia. Now I have come to help you understand what will happen to your people in the last days, for the vision refers to those days" (DANIEL 10:2–14 HCSB).

Scholars believe this messenger of God is probably an angel rather than the risen Christ. This passage shows the type of warfare in the spirit realm that the apostle Paul describes in Ephesians 6:12: "For we are not fighting against flesh-and-blood enemies, but against evil rulers and authorities of the unseen world, against mighty powers in this dark world, and against evil spirits in the heavenly places."

Now after six days Jesus took Peter, James, and John his brother, led them up on a high mountain by themselves; and

He was transfigured before them. His face shone like the sun, and His clothes became as white as the light. And behold, Moses and Elijah appeared to them, talking with Him. Then Peter answered and said to Jesus, "Lord, it is good for us to be here; if You wish, let us make here three tabernacles: one for You, one for Moses, and one for Elijah."

While he was still speaking, behold, a bright cloud overshadowed them; and suddenly a voice came out of the cloud, saying, "This is My beloved Son, in whom I am well pleased. Hear Him!" And when the disciples heard *it*, they fell on their faces and were greatly afraid. But Jesus came and touched them and said, "Arise, and do not be afraid." When they had lifted up their eyes, they saw no one but Jesus only. **(MATTHEW 17:1–8** NKJV**)**

> *The inner circle of the twelve disciples—Peter, James, and John—saw a sight few others could boast—a glimpse of the glorified Jesus and the long-dead prophets of the Old Testament: Moses and Elijah alive once more. This is Jesus between two worlds: the glorious Son of God who left his glory behind to wrap himself in human flesh. He came to fulfill the Law and the prophets, as represented by Moses and Elijah.*

And after [Jesus] had said these things, He was lifted up while they were looking on, and a cloud received Him out of their sight. And as they were gazing intently into the sky while He was going, behold, two men in white clothing stood beside them. They also said, "Men of Galilee, why do you stand looking into the sky? This Jesus, who has been taken up from you into heaven, will come in just the same way as you have watched Him go into heaven" **(ACTS 1:9–11** NASB**)**.

Jesus ascended to heaven from whence he had come and will someday return to earth.

After talking with the apostles, the Lord was taken to heaven, where God gave him the highest position. **(MARK 16:19 God's Word)**

Then Jesus took them to a place near Bethany. There he raised his hands and blessed them. While he was blessing them, he left them and was taken to heaven. **(LUKE 24:50–51 God's Word)**

The mystery that gives us our reverence for God is acknowledged to be great: He appeared in his human nature, was approved by the Spirit, was seen by angels, was announced throughout the nations, was believed in the world, and was taken to heaven in glory. **(1 TIMOTHY 3:16 God's Word)**

If ye then be risen with Christ, seek those things which are above, where Christ sitteth on the right hand of God. Set your affection on things above, not on things on the earth. For ye are dead, and your life is hid with Christ in God. When Christ, *who is* our life, shall appear, then shall ye also appear with him in glory. **(COLOSSIANS 3:1–4 kjv)**

Jesus is in a position of full authority (the right hand of the Father). When he returns to earth again, resurrected believers reflecting his glory will return with him.

"If ye then be risen with Christ" is a way of saying that believers participated in the resurrection. We died with Jesus and rose when he rose. In a sense we are between two worlds: living on earth and waiting for heaven.

But we do not want you to be uninformed, brethren, about those who are asleep, so that you will not grieve as do the rest who have no hope. For if we believe that Jesus died and rose again, even so God will bring with Him those who have fallen asleep in Jesus. For this we say to you by the word of the Lord, that we who are alive and remain until the coming of the Lord, will not precede those who have fallen asleep. For the Lord Himself will descend from heaven with a shout, with the voice of the archangel and with the trumpet of God, and the dead in Christ will rise first. Then we who are alive and remain will be caught up together with them in the clouds to meet the Lord in the air, and so we shall always be with the Lord. Therefore comfort one another with these words. **(1 THESSALONIANS 4:13–18 NASB)**

Here, Paul corrects a misconception of the Thessalonian believers. They feared that dead believers (those "who have fallen asleep") would miss out on Jesus' second coming (parousia). Paul assures them that those who are dead will be resurrected just as Jesus was resurrected. Those who are already dead will be resurrected and transformed first to meet Christ "in the air." This is known as the rapture of believers.

For Christ also suffered once for sins, the righteous for the unrighteous, that he might bring us to God, being put to death in the flesh but made alive in the spirit in which he went and proclaimed to the spirits in prison, because they formerly did not obey when God's patience waited in the days of Noah while the ark was being prepared, in which a few, that is, eight persons, were brought safely through water. . . . Jesus Christ, who has gone into heaven and is at the right hand of God, with angels, authorities, and powers having been subjected to him. . . .

For this is why the gospel was preached even to those who are dead, that though judged in the flesh the way people are, they might live in the spirit the way God does. **(1 PETER 3:18–20, 22; 4:6 ESV)**

Many scholars scramble for answers concerning this passage. Some believe that Peter is saying that Jesus went to Sheol (the realm of the dead) and preached to the people of Noah's day—the ones who were killed during the flood—after his crucifixion and before his resurrection. Others believe that the spirits mentioned in this passage are fallen angels to whom Jesus proclaimed his victory on the cross. These fallen angels are the ones mentioned in Genesis 6. Since this incident is mentioned in the epistle of Jude and 2 Peter 2:4, scholars believe that the fallen angels are indeed the spirits to whom Peter refers. Their actions contributed to the climate of sin, which led God to judge the earth. The flood was an early warning of God's judgment on the earth that would be fulfilled at the second coming of Jesus.

In 1 Peter 4:6, some scholars wonder if Peter advocates that God grants people a second chance even after they die. The concept of Purgatory sprang from the notion of an intermediary place where believers await judgment and are made fit for heaven. But the Bible never mentions Purgatory and does not seem to support this idea.

CHAPTER 5

Answers From Heaven

They say of some temporal suffering, "No future bliss can make up for it," not knowing that Heaven, once attained, will work backwards and turn even that agony into a glory.

—C. S. Lewis, *The Great Divorce*[5]

Introduction

Many prophets and ordinary people called on God for help. Some even asked for fire or judgment. Whatever they needed, they knew that God, in his heavenly realm, heard them. Often he answered by sending angels to announce glad tidings or to give God's command to go to war.

Then Sarai dealt harshly with [Hagar], and she fled from her.

The angel of the LORD found her by a spring of water in the wilderness, the spring on the way to Shur. And he said, "Hagar, servant of Sarai, where have you come from and where are you going?" She said, "I am fleeing from my mistress Sarai." The angel of the LORD said to her, "Return to your mistress and submit to her." The angel of the LORD also said to her, "I will surely multiply your offspring so that they cannot be numbered for multitude." And the angel of the LORD said to her, "Behold, you are pregnant and shall bear a son. You shall call his name Ishmael, because the LORD has listened to your affliction. He shall be a wild donkey of a man, his hand against everyone and everyone's hand against him, and he shall dwell over against all his kinsmen."

So she called the name of the LORD who spoke to her, "You are a God of seeing," for she said, "Truly here I have seen him who looks after me." Therefore the well was called Beer-lahai-roi; it lies between Kadesh and Bered. **(GENESIS 16:6–14 ESV)**

The childless Sarai (later Sarah) felt threatened by her maid Hagar. Sarai had given Hagar to Abram in order to gain children by her. Hagar fled to escape harsh treatment.

Some scholars believe that the angel of the Lord who appeared to Hagar is Christ himself. Others see the angel as a messenger sent from God with the authority to speak God's words.

And God heard the voice of the boy; and the angel of God called to Hagar from heaven, and said to her, "What troubles you, Hagar? Do not be afraid; for God has heard the voice of the boy where he is" **(GENESIS 21:17 NRSV).**

Though the sights of heaven could not be seen, God's voice could be heard from heaven. Once again, God answers Hagar when she leaves her mistress Sarah. Instead of urging her to return to Sarah, God promises Hagar that a nation of people will come from her son (21:18).

At that moment the angel of the LORD called to him from heaven, "Abraham! Abraham!"

"Yes," Abraham replied. "Here I am!"

"Don't lay a hand on the boy!" the angel said. "Do not hurt him in any way, for now I know that you truly fear God. You have not withheld from me even your son, your only son" (GENESIS 22:11–12 NLT).

Having commanded Abraham to take the son he'd waited decades for to Mount Moriah and sacrifice him, God's command rings out from heaven, staying his hand.

Then the Angel of the LORD called to Abraham a second time from heaven and said, "By Myself I have sworn, says the LORD: Because you have done this thing and have not withheld your only son, I will indeed bless you and make your offspring as numerous as the stars in the sky and the sand on the seashore. Your offspring will possess the gates of their enemies. And all the nations of the earth will be blessed by your offspring because you have obeyed My command" (GENESIS 22:15–18 HCSB).

Then the Lord told Moses to say these things to the Israelites: "You yourselves have seen that I talked with you from heaven" (EXODUS 20:22 NCV).

Here God affirms that he spoke with Moses from heaven—not from the sky. This statement was meant to remind the people of Israel not to make idols that they believe represent God.

Out of heaven he let you hear his voice, that he might discipline you. And on earth he let you see his great fire, and you heard his words out of the midst of the fire. . . . [K]now therefore today, and lay it to your heart, that the LORD is God in heaven above and on the earth beneath; there is no other. **(DEUTERONOMY 4:36, 39 ESV)**

Through Moses God attests to his authority over heaven and earth.

The LORD thundered from heaven, and the Most High uttered his voice. **(2 SAMUEL 22:14 ESV)**

David's psalm of praise (see also Psalm 18) provides many references to nature in order to describe God's power.

When Solomon finished praying, fire came down from the sky and burned up the burnt offering and the sacrifices. The LORD's glory filled the Temple. The priests could not enter the Temple of the LORD, because the LORD's glory filled it. When all the people of Israel saw the fire come down from heaven and the LORD's glory on the Temple, they bowed down on the pavement with their faces to the ground. They worshiped and thanked the LORD, saying, "He is good; his love continues forever" **(2 CHRONICLES 7:1–3 NCV).**

In answer to Solomon's prayer at the temple's dedication, God's glory not only fills the temple on earth, but fire comes down from heaven.

Then the LORD appeared to Solomon at night and said to him: I have heard your prayer and have chosen this place for Myself as a temple of sacrifice. If I close the sky so there is no rain, or if I command the grasshopper to consume the land, or if I send pestilence on My people, and My people who are called by My name humble themselves, pray and seek My face, and turn from their evil ways, then I will hear from heaven, forgive their sin, and heal their land. **(2 CHRONICLES 7:12–14 HCSB)**

Elijah replied to the captain of fifty, "If I am a man of God, let fire come down from heaven and consume you and your fifty." Then fire came down from heaven and consumed him and his fifty.

So he again sent to him another captain of fifty with his fifty. And he said to him, "O man of God, thus says the king, 'Come down quickly.' "

Elijah replied to them, "If I am a man of God, let fire come down from heaven and consume you and your fifty." Then the fire of God came down from heaven and consumed him and his fifty.

So he again sent the captain of a third fifty with his fifty. When the third captain of fifty went up, he came and bowed down on his knees before Elijah, and begged him and said to him, "O man of God, please let my life and the lives of these fifty servants of yours be precious in your sight.

"Behold fire came down from heaven and consumed the first two captains of fifty with their fifties; but now let my life be precious in your sight."

The angel of the LORD said to Elijah, "Go down with him; do not be afraid of him." So he arose and went down with him to the king. **(2 KINGS 1:10–15 NASB)**

King Ahaziah, an idol worshiper, had injured himself, and Elijah had prophesied that he would die in his bed. Ahaziah

*sent messengers to bring Elijah to him. But just as God
answered the prophet Elijah by sending fire from heaven on
Mount Carmel (1 Kings 18:36–38), he again sends fire in
recognition of the prophet's prayer.*

———◆———

But King Hezekiah and Isaiah the prophet, the son of Amoz,
prayed about this and cried out to heaven. And the LORD sent
an angel who destroyed every mighty warrior, commander
and officer in the camp of the king of Assyria. So he returned
in shame to his own land. And when he had entered the
temple of his god, some of his own children killed him there
with the sword. **(2 CHRONICLES 32:20–21 NASB)**

*Sennacherib, king of the Assyrians, attacked the nation of
Judah. He doubted the ability of the God of Israel to stop his
seemingly unstoppable army. Yet one angel killed 185,000
soldiers. This king, Sennacherib, found justice at the hands
of his own children.*

———◆———

You alone are the LORD. You made the skies and the heavens and all the stars. You made the earth and the seas and
everything in them. You preserve them all, and the angels of
heaven worship you. . . . You came down at Mount Sinai and
spoke to them from heaven. You gave them regulations and
instructions that were just, and decrees and commands that
were good. . . . You gave them bread from heaven when they
were hungry and water from the rock when they were thirsty.
You commanded them to go and take possession of the land
you had sworn to give them. . . . So you handed them over
to their enemies, who made them suffer. But in their time of
trouble they cried to you, and you heard them from heaven.

In your great mercy, you sent them liberators who rescued them from their enemies.

But as soon as they were at peace, your people again committed evil in your sight, and once more you let their enemies conquer them. Yet whenever your people turned and cried to you again for help, you listened once more from heaven. In your wonderful mercy, you rescued them many times! **(NEHEMIAH 9:6, 13, 15, 27–28 NLT)**

During a prayer of confession after the rebuilding of the walls of Jerusalem, a group of Levites recount the many ways God has answered his people.

Now I know that the LORD gives victory to His anointed; He will answer him from His holy heaven with mighty victories from His right hand. **(PSALM 20:6 HCSB)**

In the first part of this psalm (written by David), the people talk to the king. Here King David ("His anointed") praises God for his answers.

From heaven you pronounced judgment, and the land feared and was quiet—when you, O God, rose up to judge, to save all the afflicted of the land. Selah. **(PSALM 76:8–9 NIV)**

This is probably a reference to God's deliverance of Judah from the Assyrians led by Sennacherib during the reign of King Hezekiah (2 Kings 19:35; 2 Chronicles 32:20–21).

While the words were still in the king's mouth, a voice came from heaven: "King Nebuchadnezzar, to you it is declared that the kingdom has departed from you. You will be driven away from people to live with the wild animals, and you will feed on grass like cattle for seven periods of time, until you acknowledge that the Most High is ruler over the kingdom of men, and He gives it to anyone He wants" **(DANIEL 4:31–32 HCSB)**.

God speaks to King Nebuchadnezzar of Babylon from heaven in response to Nebuchadnezzar's arrogance. Having given him a dream that required interpreting by Daniel, God now pronounces judgment against Nebuchadnezzar.

After Jesus was baptized, He went up immediately from the water. The heavens suddenly opened for Him, and He saw the Spirit of God descending like a dove and coming down on Him. And there came a voice from heaven: This is My beloved Son. I take delight in Him! **(MATTHEW 3:16–17 HCSB)**

And in the same region there were shepherds out in the field, keeping watch over their flock by night. And an angel of the Lord appeared to them, and the glory of the Lord shone around them, and they were filled with fear. And the angel said to them, "Fear not, for behold, I bring you good news of great joy that will be for all the people. For unto you is born this day in the city of David a Savior, who is Christ the Lord. And this will be a sign for you: you will find a baby wrapped in swaddling cloths and lying in a manger." And suddenly there was with the angel a multitude of the heavenly host praising God and saying, "Glory to God in the highest, and on earth peace among those with whom he is pleased!"

When the angels went away from them into heaven, the shepherds said to one another, "Let us go over to Bethlehem and see this thing that has happened, which the Lord has made known to us" **(LUKE 2:8–15 ESV).**

"Father, give glory to your name." A voice from heaven said, "I have given it glory, and I will give it glory again" **(JOHN 12:28 GOD'S WORD).**

Once more God speaks audibly from heaven to affirm his Son and the plan to which God and his Son agreed.

Suddenly a sound like the blowing of a violent wind came from heaven and filled the whole house where they were sitting. They saw what seemed to be tongues of fire that separated and came to rest on each of them.

All of them were filled with the Holy Spirit and began to speak in other tongues as the Spirit enabled them. **(ACTS 2:2–4 NIV)**

After Jesus ascended into heaven, the Holy Spirit was sent from heaven to live within each believer on earth.

As he neared Damascus on his journey, suddenly a light from heaven flashed around him.

He fell to the ground and heard a voice say to him, "Saul, Saul, why do you persecute me?"

"Who are you, Lord?" Saul asked. "I am Jesus, whom you are persecuting," he replied. "Now get up and go into the city, and you will be told what you must do" **(ACTS 9:3–6 NIV).**

Saul of Tarsus, the zealous persecutor of believers, encounters the risen Christ, who spoke to him from heaven. In

other passages (Acts 22:6–11; 26:13–20; 1 Corinthians 9:1;
15:8; Galatians 1:16), Saul, who later became known by his
Roman name, Paul, admits that he saw the risen Christ. This
encounter changed his life forever.

Then he became very hungry and wanted to eat; but while
they made ready, he fell into a trance and saw heaven opened
and an object like a great sheet bound at the four corners,
descending to him and let down to the earth. In it were all
kinds of four-footed animals of the earth, wild beasts, creep-
ing things, and birds of the air.

And a voice came to him, "Rise, Peter; kill and eat."

But Peter said, "Not so, Lord! For I have never eaten
anything common or unclean."

And a voice spoke to him again the second time, "What
God has cleansed you must not call common."

This was done three times. And the object was taken up
into heaven again. **(ACTS 10:10–16 NKJV)** (See also Acts 11:5–10.)

Peter saw a vision showing the unclean food listed in Leviti-
cus 11. But this answer from heaven was not about food per
se, but about a people considered unclean—Gentiles. Peter
would soon have a close encounter with a Gentile named
Cornelius. This was God's way of saying that the door to
heaven was now open to Gentiles.

God's anger is revealed from heaven against every ungodly
and immoral thing people do as they try to suppress the truth
by their immoral living. **(ROMANS 1:18 GOD'S WORD)**

CHAPTER 6

Who Will Go to Heaven?

*All their life in this world and all their adventures in
Narnia had only been the cover and the title page: now at
last they were beginning Chapter One of the Great Story,
which no one on earth has read: which goes on for ever:
in which every chapter is better than the one before.*

—C. S. Lewis, *The Last Battle*[6]

Introduction

Edward Hicks, a Quaker minister living in Pennsylvania in
1780–1849, is well known for his series of *Peaceable Kingdom*
paintings. These paintings, begun around 1820, were inspired
by the prophecies of Isaiah 11. Looking at the paintings, which
feature children and peaceful animals, one can't help asking,
"Will there really be animals in heaven?" But an even more important question is "Which *people* can go there?" Many Scriptures explain who will and who won't be found in heaven.

But as for me, I know that my Redeemer lives, and he will
stand upon the earth at last.

And after my body has decayed, yet in my body I will see God! (JOB 19:25–26 NLT)

Job believes that the One referred to as the Redeemer of Israel (Isaiah 43:19) will vindicate him. Scholars, however, argue whether or not Job believed that vindication would come after death (in heaven).

———◆———

Not everyone who says to Me, "Lord, Lord," will enter the kingdom of heaven, but he who does the will of My Father who is in heaven will enter. Many will say to Me on that day, "Lord, Lord, did we not prophesy in Your name, and in Your name cast out demons, and in Your name perform many miracles?" And then I will declare to them, "I never knew you; DEPART FROM ME, YOU WHO PRACTICE LAWLESS-NESS" (MATTHEW 7:21–23 NASB).

"That day" refers to the day of judgment after the second coming of Christ. This chilling message is a warning against fake disciples and prophets. They will find the doors of heaven closed to them.

———◆———

I tell you, many will come from east and west and recline at table with Abraham, Isaac, and Jacob in the kingdom of heaven, while the sons of the kingdom will be thrown into the outer darkness. In that place there will be weeping and gnashing of teeth. (MATTHEW 8:11–12 ESV)

Here Jesus refers to the great banquet or "marriage supper of the lamb" discussed in Revelation 19:9 (see chapter 2). Those not invited will face great suffering.

———◆———

Whoever acknowledges me before men, I will also acknowledge him before my Father in heaven. But whoever disowns me before men, I will disown him before my Father in heaven. (MATTHEW 10:32–33 NIV)

And Jesus answered and spoke to them again by parables and said: "The kingdom of heaven is like a certain king who arranged a marriage for his son, and sent out his servants to call those who were invited to the wedding; and they were not willing to come. Again, he sent out other servants, saying, 'Tell those who are invited, "See, I have prepared my dinner; my oxen and fatted cattle are killed, and all things are ready. Come to the wedding." ' But they made light of it and went their ways, one to his own farm, another to his business. And the rest seized his servants, treated them spitefully, and killed them. But when the king heard about it, he was furious. And he sent out his armies, destroyed those murderers, and burned up their city. Then he said to his servants, 'The wedding is ready, but those who were invited were not worthy. Therefore go into the highways, and as many as you find, invite to the wedding.' So those servants went out into the highways and gathered together all whom they found, both bad and good. And the wedding hall was filled with guests.

"But when the king came in to see the guests, he saw a man there who did not have on a wedding garment. So he said to him, 'Friend, how did you come in here without a wedding garment?' And he was speechless. Then the king said to the servants, 'Bind him hand and foot, take him away, and cast him into outer darkness; there will be weeping and gnashing of teeth.'

"For many are called, but few are chosen" (MATTHEW 22:1–14 NKJV).

Although Jesus used a parable, this appears to be the marriage supper of the Lamb described in Revelation 19:6–9 and foretold in Isaiah 25:6–9. Many scholars believe this feast will take place during the millennial rule of Jesus. Guests are invited to come by invitation of the Savior, whose righteousness provides the wedding garment—the new life created by the Holy Spirit. Those without the Holy Spirit will not remain. The man without a wedding garment is a person who is not clothed in the righteousness of Christ.

The first invited guests were the people of Israel. Afterward, the invitation to the heavenly banquet was extended to Gentiles.

———— ◆ • ————

The same day some Sadducees, who say there is no resurrection, came up to Him and questioned Him: "Teacher, Moses said, if a man dies, having no children, his brother is to marry his wife and raise up offspring for his brother. Now there were seven brothers among us. The first got married and died. Having no offspring, he left his wife to his brother. The same happened to the second also, and the third, and so to all seven. Then last of all the woman died. Therefore, in the resurrection, whose wife will she be of the seven? For they all had married her."

Jesus answered them, "You are deceived, because you don't know the Scriptures or the power of God. For in the resurrection they neither marry nor are given in marriage but are like angels in heaven. Now concerning the resurrection of the dead, haven't you read what was spoken to you by God: I am the God of Abraham and the God of Isaac and the God of Jacob? He is not the God of the dead, but of the living."

And when the crowds heard this, they were astonished at His teaching. **(MATTHEW 22:23–33 HCSB)**

Jesus always knew when a trap had been laid for him, and the Sadducees' question was merely a trap, since they didn't believe in the resurrection to come.

Jesus' statement that people will be like angels does not mean that people will become angels in heaven. It merely means that no one will get married in heaven, just as the angels do not marry.

Then the kingdom of heaven will be like 10 virgins who took their lamps and went out to meet the groom. Five of them were foolish and five were sensible. When the foolish took their lamps, they didn't take oil with them. But the sensible ones took oil in their flasks with their lamps. Since the groom was delayed, they all became drowsy and fell asleep.

In the middle of the night there was a shout: "Here's the groom! Come out to meet him."

Then all those virgins got up and trimmed their lamps. But the foolish ones said to the sensible ones, "Give us some of your oil, because our lamps are going out."

The sensible ones answered, "No, there won't be enough for us and for you. Go instead to those who sell, and buy oil for yourselves."

When they had gone to buy some, the groom arrived. Then those who were ready went in with him to the wedding banquet, and the door was shut.

Later the rest of the virgins also came and said, "Master, master, open up for us!"

But he replied, "I assure you: I do not know you!"

Therefore be alert, because you don't know either the day or the hour. **(MATTHEW 25:1–13 HCSB)**

Chapter 25 of Matthew is part of Jesus' Olivet Discourse. (See chapter 24 in chapter 2.) This is the first of three stories Jesus used to illustrate the kingdom of heaven.

Here Jesus tells the parable of the ten bridesmaids as a warning to be ready for his second coming. He used the Jewish wedding custom to illustrate his point. The bridegroom usually proceeded to the bride's home to take her to the wedding. Jesus is the bridegroom, a metaphor discussed in Isaiah 54:4–6 and confirmed by Jesus in Mark 2:19–20. The bridesmaids represent the expectant disciples. But note that the bridesmaids were shut out of the wedding banquet. This banquet is the marriage supper of the lamb (Revelation 19:9; see also Matthew 22:1–14 above).

For [the kingdom of heaven] is like a man who was about to take a long journey, and he called his servants together and entrusted them with his property. To one he gave five talents [probably about $5,000], to another two, to another one—to each in proportion to his own personal ability. Then he departed and left the country.

He who had received the five talents went at once and traded with them, and he gained five talents more. And likewise he who had received the two talents—he also gained two talents more. But he who had received the one talent went and dug a hole in the ground and hid his master's money.

Now after a long time the master of those servants returned and settled accounts with them. And he who had received the five talents came and brought him five more, saying, Master, you entrusted to me five talents; see, here I have gained five talents more.

His master said to him, Well done, you upright (honorable, admirable) and faithful servant! You have been faithful and trustworthy over a little; I will put you in charge of much.

Enter into and share the joy (the delight, the blessedness) which your master enjoys.

And he also who had the two talents came forward, saying, Master, you entrusted two talents to me; here I have gained two talents more.

His master said to him, Well done, you upright (honorable, admirable) and faithful servant! You have been faithful and trustworthy over a little; I will put you in charge of much. Enter into and share the joy (the delight, the blessedness) which your master enjoys.

He who had received one talent also came forward, saying, Master, I knew you to be a harsh and hard man, reaping where you did not sow, and gathering where you had not winnowed [the grain].

So I was afraid, and I went and hid your talent in the ground. Here you have what is your own.

But his master answered him, You wicked and lazy and idle servant! Did you indeed know that I reap where I have not sowed and gather [grain] where I have not winnowed?

Then you should have invested my money with the bankers, and at my coming I would have received what was my own with interest.

So take the talent away from him and give it to the one who has the ten talents.

For to everyone who has will more be given, and he will be furnished richly so that he will have an abundance; but from the one who does not have, even what he does have will be taken away.

And throw the good-for-nothing servant into the outer darkness; there will be weeping and grinding of teeth. **(MATTHEW 25:14–30 AMP)**

This is the second of three parables of the kingdom of heaven. This parable is about faithfulness in stewardship. What one does with one's God-given resources in this life will be judged and rewarded by God. "Outer darkness" is a euphemism for hell or damnation.

But when the Son of Man comes in his glory, and all the angels with him, then he will sit upon his glorious throne. All the nations will be gathered in his presence, and he will separate the people as a shepherd separates the sheep from the goats. He will place the sheep at his right hand and the goats at his left.

Then the King will say to those on his right, "Come, you who are blessed by my Father, inherit the Kingdom prepared for you from the creation of the world. For I was hungry, and you fed me. I was thirsty, and you gave me a drink. I was a stranger, and you invited me into your home. I was naked, and you gave me clothing. I was sick, and you cared for me. I was in prison, and you visited me."

Then these righteous ones will reply, "Lord, when did we ever see you hungry and feed you? Or thirsty and give you something to drink? Or a stranger and show you hospitality? Or naked and give you clothing? When did we ever see you sick or in prison and visit you?"

And the King will say, "I tell you the truth, when you did it to one of the least of these my brothers and sisters, you were doing it to me!"

Then the King will turn to those on the left and say, "Away with you, you cursed ones, into the eternal fire prepared for the devil and his demons. For I was hungry, and you didn't feed me. I was thirsty, and you didn't give me a drink. I was a stranger, and you didn't invite me into your home. I was naked, and you didn't give me clothing. I was sick and in prison, and you didn't visit me."

Then they will reply, "Lord, when did we ever see you hungry or thirsty or a stranger or naked or sick or in prison, and not help you?"

And he will answer, "I tell you the truth, when you refused to help the least of these my brothers and sisters, you were refusing to help me."

And they will go away into eternal punishment, but the righteous will go into eternal life. (MATTHEW 25:31–46 NLT)

This is the third of three parables of the kingdom of heaven.

──── ◆ ────

Jesus looked around and said to his disciples, "How hard it will be for rich people to enter the kingdom of God!"

The disciples were stunned by his words. But Jesus said to them again, "Children, how hard it is to enter the kingdom of God! It is easier for a camel to go through the eye of a needle than for a rich person to enter the kingdom of God."

This amazed his disciples more than ever. They asked each other, "Who, then, can be saved?"

Jesus looked at them and said, "It's impossible for people to save themselves, but it's not impossible for God to save them. Everything is possible for God" (MARK 10:23–27 GOD'S WORD).

──── ◆ ────

For God loved the world so much that he gave his one and only Son, so that everyone who believes in him will not perish but have eternal life. (JOHN 3:16 NLT)

When another prominent individual (Nicodemus) appeared before Jesus, the Savior explained the plan of salvation—the only way to heaven.

But this is what the Scripture says about being made right through faith: "Don't say to yourself, 'Who will go up into heaven?' " (That means, "Who will go up to heaven and bring Christ down to earth?") "And do not say, 'Who will go down into the world below?' " (That means, "Who will go down and bring Christ up from the dead?") This is what the Scripture says: "The word is near you; it is in your mouth and in your heart." That is the teaching of faith that we are telling. (ROMANS 10:6–8 NCV)

Paul repeats the words that Moses used in Deuteronomy 30:12–14. Just as Moses assured the people of Israel that there was no excuse not to obey the law, Paul mentions that Christ has already come to earth to fulfill the law. So there was even less of an excuse to doubt Christ. In either case, humility is the key to a heart willing to obey.

Now, therefore, you are no longer strangers and foreigners, but fellow citizens with the saints and members of the household of God. (EPHESIANS 2:19 NKJV)

But our citizenship is in heaven, and from it we await a Savior, the Lord Jesus Christ, who will transform our lowly body to be like his glorious body, by the power that enables him even to subject all things to himself. (PHILIPPIANS 3:20–21 ESV)

Beloved, we are God's children now, and what we will be has not yet appeared; but we know that when he appears

we shall be like him, because we shall see him as he is.
(1 JOHN 3:2 ESV)

⸺ ◈ ⸺

I've written this to those who believe in the Son of God so
that they will know that they have eternal life. **(1 JOHN 5:13
GOD'S WORD)**

> *As the apostle John also mentioned in his gospel (John
> 20:30), the Scriptures have one purpose: to encourage belief
> in the Son of God.*
>
> *Heaven is within the grasp of anyone. All it takes to enter
> is one step toward the Son of God. Have you taken that step?*

NOTES

1. Elizabeth Goudge, *The Valley of Song* (New York: Coward-McCann, 1951), 31.

2. From Canto I of *Paradiso* in *The Divine Comedy* by Dante Alighieri, *www.readprint.com/chapter-190/Paradiso-Dante-Alighieri* (accessed April 14, 2011).

3. From "Part I: The Tenth Stage" of *The Pilgrim's Progress* by John Bunyan. Quoted at Christian Classics Ethereal Library, *www.ccel.org/ccel/bunyan/pilgrim* (accessed April 14, 2011).

4. From Canto V of *Purgatorio* in *The Divine Comedy* by Dante Alighieri, *www.readprint.com/chapter-227/Purgatorio-Dante-Alighieri*, accessed April 14, 2011.

5. From *The Great Divorce* in *The Best of C. S. Lewis* (New York: The Iversen Associates, 1969), 153.

6. C. S. Lewis, *The Last Battle* (New York: Collier Books/Macmillan Publishing Company, 1956), 184.

Books in This Series

Everything the Bible Says About Prayer
Everything the Bible Says About Heaven
Everything the Bible Says About Money
Everything the Bible Says About Angels and Demons